Geoffrey Boycott joined the Yorkshire team in 1962. Two years later he was picked for England, making his first Test hundred at the Oval. His 146 not out in 1965 remains the highest score ever made in a Gillette Cup final. In 1971 and 1979 he averaged over one hundred for the season – the only player ever to do this twice. He captained England four times in 1977 and 1978. In 1977 he scored his hundredth first-class hundred at the Headingley Test match, and in 1980 he was awarded the OBE. Captain of Yorkshire from 1971 to 1978, he was finally driven out of the side at the end of 1986. Both *Boycott: An Autobiography*, published in 1987, and *Boycott on Cricket*, published in 1990, immediately became number one hardcover bestsellers. *Boycott: An Autobiography* is also available in paperback from Corgi.

Front cover photo
by Patrick Eagar

D1150758

Also by Geoffrey Boycott
BOYCOTT: AN AUTOBIOGRAPHY
and published by Corgi Books

BOYCOTT ON CRICKET

Geoffrey Boycott

CORGI BOOKS

BOYCOTT ON CRICKET
A CORGI BOOK 0 552 99448 0

Originally published in Great Britain by Partridge Press,
a division of Transworld Publishers Ltd

PRINTING HISTORY
Partridge Press edition published 1990
Corgi edition published 1991

This book is set in Baskerville by
Chippendale Type Ltd., Otley, West Yorkshire.

Corgi Books are published by Transworld Publishers
Ltd., 61–63 Uxbridge Road, Ealing, London W5 5SA, in
Australia by Transworld Publishers (Australia) Pty. Ltd.,
15–23 Helles Avenue, Moorebank, NSW 2170, and in New
Zealand by Transworld Publishers (N.Z.) Ltd., Cnr. Moselle
and Waipareira Avenues, Henderson, Auckland.

Made and printed in Great Britain by
Cox & Wyman Ltd., Reading, Berks.

CONTENTS

Acknowledgement

My thanks and appreciation to John Callaghan for his help and contribution in the writing of my book.

1

England in decline?

England entered the 1990s with a dreadful record, having been victors in only one of their previous twenty-five Tests and that against Sri Lanka, who could hardly be described as formidable opposition. Following defeat at the hands of a well-organized, determined Australian team the England players were demoralized and there was a widely held view that it would be better to abandon the proposed West Indies tour to avoid further humiliation. Preparations for the Caribbean began under a cloud, with selection for the trip being regarded as the equivalent of the death sentence.

One of the first things that Ted Dexter said on being appointed to his £30,000-a-year post as chairman of the selectors was that he hoped I would help with the batting, a comment which sparked a lot of newspaper speculation and left me in an embarrassing position. For the record, I did meet Dexter three times during the summer, but each time the only subject of conversation was golf, so I stood back and sadly followed events from a distance. Only at the end of the season did Micky Stewart, the England manager, telephone me to suggest that the batsmen chosen for the West Indies and the 'A' team trip to Zimbabwe would benefit from my guidance in the course of some intensive coaching sessions. I agreed to do what I could, although I stressed from the start that I did not intend to waste my time talking to players who did not want to listen. The crucial point about coaching is that those on the receiving end must have complete faith in the person handing out advice if a meaningful relationship is to be established. On that basis I have always been happy to talk about the technicalities of batting to anyone. I suppose in a small way I did contribute to our Ashes disappointment in 1989 by improving the attitude and technique of Australian Dean Jones during the previous year. I was pleased to help him, because he asked me.

Cricket had been a joke 'down under', with the national team stumbling in utter confusion from one defeat to the next. In stopping the rot, Bobby Simpson, a down-to-earth former batsman and captain of the old school, adopted an uncompromising attitude as manager. He picked out players he believed had talent and mental toughness, ironed out their weaknesses and got them back to basics. Building on that, he arranged for training sessions before every Test at which players had to stretch themselves, so that when it came to the crunch each individual was in a position to do himself justice. In comparison, England under David Gower's captaincy had settled for desultory practice sessions and pleasing themselves about the way in which they prepared.

I played the last of my 108 Tests against India in 1982 and when I returned home ill from Calcutta the bulk of the tabloid press reported that the rest of the party were glad to see the back of me. 'Now the England tourists can enjoy their cricket,' proclaimed one, but the dedication and professionalism for which I attracted so much criticism were the qualities England lacked, as their stock sank lower and lower. As standards declined and the walls of self-satisfaction crashed down around his head, Peter May, chairman of selectors before Dexter, admitted that the wheel had turned full circle. Speaking after a crushing Headingley defeat by India in 1986 he said: 'Our batsmen are unable to sustain a long innings. We desperately need players who can maintain their concentration throughout a full day to make a big score. Too many in the team look anxiously at the scoreboard, see that they have not made a run for ten minutes or so and do something rash.'

The statistics of that Leeds game make grim reading, for England was bowled out for 102 and 128 by a far-from-ferocious attack, in which Roger Binny's gentle medium pace claimed match figures of 7–58. England was beaten by 279 runs in little more than three days, despite playing six specialist batsmen. The selectors were frantically seeking a reliable opening partner for Graham Gooch and actually used three – Tim Robinson, Wilf Slack and Mark Benson – in as many matches against the Indians. It was all too much for one Yorkshire member. Spotting Fred Titmus at Headingley, he marched up to the former Middlesex and England off-spinner, who was in his first spell as a selector, and told him that I was the man they needed. 'Boycott has all the necessary skill, concentration and application,' he insisted. Titmus replied: 'We aren't playing a ten-day Test, you know.' 'You're right,' said the member. 'We can't even last four days.' Titmus was left to beat a hasty retreat.

Throughout my international career I appreciated the value of occupying the crease, of grinding down the opposition and of taking out insurance against the possibility of defeat before going on to try to win. There is an old saying in cricket that bowlers win matches, but it is no more than a superficial half-truth, a misrepresentation of the real situation. In Test cricket batting is the key – if you don't score enough runs you aren't in the game. Batsmen create the circumstances in which bowlers, who admittedly do have to capture twenty wickets, can exert their influence. A side batting first in a five-day Test should always aim to

3

use up most of the first two days in compiling a very big total. Nothing less than 350 is acceptable and something around 500 is much better, because it puts the match out of reach of the opposition who know then that they have to spend the next three days engaged in a rearguard action. It is a matter of simple mathematics.

The game suffered from an obsession with 'brighter cricket' in the 1960s, when virtually every touring captain made a facile promise his players could not hope to keep. England dropped me in 1967 for slow scoring at Headingley when I reached 246 not out against India, yet, although I was not in anything like form, 106 came on the first day – a rate of progress that in the 1970s and 1980s would have been a godsend.

Recently, I have noticed that many of the batsmen reaching the England side and, in some cases, staying in it, were being handicapped by major weaknesses in technique. A few examples, covering a cross-section of those prominent on the domestic scene will illustrate the extent of the problem.

Tim Curtis The thirty-year-old Worcestershire opener has a lot of pluses, including a good temperament, plenty of concentration and a strong desire to do well, so it is a pity that his technique is so badly flawed. Having spent so much of his career at New Road, where the pitches are on the quick side, Curtis instinctively stays back and picks up a lot of his runs with the pull and the cut. His weight automatically goes on to the back foot, so he pushes forward very rarely and, when he does get on to the front foot, he has a very short stride. The natural arc of his bat comes from gulley to mid-wicket, which forces him to play across the line of the ball. Seamers do pitch that little bit shorter at Worcester, which enables him to get away with the cut and the pull and, once he settles in, he scores steadily. His favourite horizontal strokes make great use of the right hand, but when it comes to playing

4

forward he does not get the left elbow and shoulder into his shots enough and so finds enormous difficulty in playing straight. Test match bowlers are not fools and they can see that Curtis is vulnerable to well pitched-up deliveries, so they exploit this. Until he sorts out the problem I have described, Curtis will never be more than an adequate county cricketer.

Kim Barnett has a lot of shot-making ability, but just before the bowler lets go of the ball his right leg slides back and outside the line of the leg stump. From that one movement he is in trouble. He puts himself further away from his stumps and has to move into the ball at an angle of forty-five degrees. The thirty-year-old Derbyshire captain has been criticized for playing around his front leg, but he cannot do anything else once he has made that initial movement which turns his body round, pointing at mid-off. To deal with a straight delivery it is difficult for him to bring the bat down straight, so he must literally swing it in a semi-circular motion around his pad towards mid-wicket. Also, because he is a long way from the ball he cannot keep his balance, so when he plays forward he has to move his left foot twice. Every problem stems from that error before the bowler has even delivered the ball.

Graham Gooch   A basic initial mistake is at the heart of his difficulties also. When playing forward he plants his left foot on the line of the ball, thus forcing himself to bring the bat around his front pad when he tries to play the ball. If the ball moves into him, he has to play even further around his pad and follow the ball. That is the only way he can hope to make contact, but it gives him little chance of playing straight. Gooch's problem is accentuated because he has always batted in an upright manner with what I call a stiff left leg, which bends only slightly at the knee. The art of batting is to put your left foot inside or next to the line of the ball so that the bat can come down straight next to the pad. Gooch must make a conscious effort to bend his left knee a lot more so that the weight of his body moves forward, bringing his head over the ball.

He has escaped some of the consequences of poor technique when batting on good pitches that allow limited movement of the ball. Against the West Indian pace bowlers, who hurry the ball on to him, his power has served him well and he averages 41.81. In contrast he has had little success against Australia in England, averaging 27.19 from forty-seven innings. The Australian bowlers are more subtle, using swing, seam and change of pace while varying the angle of attack to put a premium on technical skill.

Robert Bailey is a batsman with lots of determination who is as keen as mustard to do well and plays nicely enough at times, but he looks like a complete novice when the ball does anything on or around the line of the off stump. Sometimes he misses it by four or five inches, which is ridiculous for a good batsman. Sitting at home watching the 1987 Benson and Hedges Cup Final between Yorkshire and Northamptonshire, I could not believe how badly Bailey fared against Paul Jarvis, being beaten so often that it must have come as a relief when he finally edged one and got out. The incredible point was that no-one had told him what he was doing wrong until he spoke to me, even though the fault was so simple. When I played forward my left toe pointed to extra cover, thus keeping my body sideways to the bowler. When Bailey played forward his left foot opened up, so that his toe pointed straight back down the pitch. The effect was to turn his body open or 'chest on'. This meant he was driving at the ball without his body, using only his hands. His bat came down towards mid-wicket when he thought he was playing straight. The ball moving away towards the slips passed his bat travelling in almost the opposite direction. The chances of the two objects meeting were slim in the extreme and, at best,

Bailey could expect to do little more than deflect the ball into the slips. Even when the ball went through straight, he was likely to slice it anywhere in an arc between cover and backward point, for he had no real control.

The tragedy is that Bailey, who probably started playing cricket like most of us at nine or ten, reached the age of twenty-six before I told him why he could not play consistently and safely through the off side. Just by pointing his toe in the wrong direction he removed the left hand of his body from the shot, hitting exclusively with his right hand, yet batting is all about the left side – left shoulder, left elbow, left hand.

Nasser Hussain   This boy, at twenty-one, is regarded as one of England's brightest prospects and he earned selection for the West Indies tour over other highly rated youngsters like Michael Atherton and Mark Ramprakash. He has some nice touches, but is certainly not as polished as Colin Cowdrey, Peter May or Ted Dexter were when they came down from university. He arrived at the nets in the build-up to the West Indies tour terribly naïve, so I attempted to explain to him what batting is all about in the Caribbean. I emphasized that as West Indian bowlers are going to get the average batsman out with unplayable deliveries four or five times in a series, the last thing he can afford to do is to give away his wicket. I stressed that the careful selection of each stroke was vital, so, with the nets pulled back and Jack Russell keeping wicket to simulate conditions in the middle, he applied himself for a spell against Devon Malcolm, Angus Fraser, Ricardo Ellcock and Gladstone Small. Suddenly, however, he flashed outside the off stump off the back foot and edged to what would have been first slip. Two or three balls later he repeated the mistake and finally he lunged wildly at one so wide that his mum could not have reached it with her broom!

When I asked him pretty bluntly what he thought he was doing, he said: 'Well, I get a lot of runs through

7

there,' indicating with a sweep of his arm the area between cover and cover-point. 'I feel that if I don't play through there I won't score at all.' Trying to put his concern into perspective, I posed another question. 'How many fours do you think you have hit in the fifteen minutes or so you've been batting?' 'Three, maybe four,' he replied. 'Fine,' I told him. 'I know you've been caught at slip twice and, when you went to force off the back foot, you were a bit late and the ball slipped off the face of the bat to gulley. That was not a bad shot technically, but you played it to the wrong ball. I'll forget the one you missed from Devon Malcolm that knocked your stumps over, although that was criminal because you let a straight delivery bowl you. Allowing for that loss of concentration and giving you one or two runs for the odd single you might have picked up, your average is five or six runs per innings. You're playing as though you're still at university, crashing little medium-pacers all over the field.' It was immature and undisciplined. To add to the problem, his stance had also been neglected. Hussain stands 'sideways on' with his feet, but he turns his right shoulder into a very open 'chest on' position, allowing the bowler to see all his right side. Presumably no-one at university had told him, but the fact is that as long as Hussain remains open chested he is always likely to slice any delivery of slightly extra pace or bounce off the face of the bat to the slips or gulley area – just as he did in the nets when accentuating the fault by trying to force the ball and maintain some imaginary run rate in his head.

Hussain has received a lot of praise for his ability to raise the tempo in one-day matches and run-chases by opening the face of the bat to slide the ball through the vacant gulley area. The same stroke in a Test match, against the new ball or against a high-quality fast bowler in championship cricket, will result in catching practice for the close cordon of slip fielders. Unless he alters, word will go round that Hussain has this weakness and captains will be happy to give him a few runs in his favourite area in exchange for his wicket. In my first Test series in 1964 Bobby Simpson caught me at slip three times off Graham Corling and told me: 'You keep edging them, Geoffrey, and I'll keep catching them.' I decided that the profitable thing to do was to work out a way to stop edging them – and I did. Hussain may have to learn the hard way, too.

Michael Atherton   Right from the start Atherton had lovely balanced feet, but he got them in the wrong position. He took guard with his feet outside the leg stump, giving the bowler a full view of all the stumps. When playing back, Atherton pushed his right foot either straight back or further to the leg side, leaving his stumps unprotected. On the other hand, when he went forward to a ball pitched up on or around his off stump, Atherton's left foot had such a long way to go towards the ball that it got only just in front of the batting crease. Although he opened his legs and got a good stride, it was of little benefit to him because it took him sideways rather than down the pitch. Good foot movement takes the batsman right forward to get as near as possible to the pitch of the ball, or right back to protect the stumps. Atherton did not achieve either objective. During the build-up to the 'A' team tour to Zimbabwe, I got Atherton to put his right foot back and into the stumps to cover them. This meant that when he played forward he was aiming straight down the pitch towards the bowler and also making a worthwhile stride towards the ball.

I found it hard to accept that I was working with the best batsmen in the country when I supervised my first net session for the England squad, and, inevitably, it was impossible to do little more than scratch the surface in the time available. I had only a handful of sessions with the batsmen, so all I could do for those in the party for the West Indies was to identify their strengths and weaknesses and point them in the right direction. I had to hope that somehow in the heat of battle the odd tip would provide some comfort. Technical faults were so deeply ingrained that they could not be cured overnight. Months of concentrated effort was really needed and, while the response from the players was tremendous, I realized that under pressure, with the ball whizzing around their ears at ninety miles an hour, the batsmen would probably revert to their old ways. West Indian bowlers are not exactly noted for giving the opposition scope to think carefully about what they are doing and a perfect technique has to be honed over a long period so that it becomes second nature. The key is muscle memory, which can be achieved only after many hours of hard work.

When Nick Faldo made the slight adjustment to his back swing he knew he would have to do more than just hit balls until he got into a smooth groove on the practice ground. He understood that he would have some anxious moments in major competitions and be tempted to abandon his new method before the reshaped swing became automatic. In this way golf and batting are much the same. The player cannot afford to be thinking about the mechanics of his game when he should be concentrating on the ball. During the coaching sessions with England I did not attempt to make the batsmen into carbon copies of myself. That has never been my way. Nor did I advocate that they should play only one or two particular strokes and cut out the rest, or that they should be ultra-defensive. Instead I underlined how vital it would be for them to be selective in their shot-making in order to minimize the risk factors. I advised the England batsmen to give a lot of thought to each innings, pointing out that it is fatal to worry about run-rates in the West Indies, where an individual is likely to be rationed to around seventy-two deliveries in a full session. Of these at least a third will be short and lifting, or wide. With a bit of luck about forty will be in the target area and, on a good day, the batsman may make slightly more than a run from every two of these balls, which gives him between twenty and twenty-five runs in two hours. That sort of score may not seem very much, but it is nothing to be ashamed about, and it is much better to be twenty-five not out than to be sitting in the dressing-room after getting out to an irresponsible shot.

I also warned the tourists to remember that all their mistakes would be captured by the camera to be shown on television at home, accompanied by predictable press criticism. It is not fair to put too much blame on young shoulders. England lack battle-hardened professionals of the calibre of Ken Barrington and John Edrich. Hussain and Atherton are victims of circumstance and of a pathetic coaching system that sends them into action ill prepared. Hussain set out for the West Indies a novice and Atherton was in exactly the same position when he made his Test debut against Australia in 1989: in each case the selectors and many cricket enthusiasts were expecting miracles. Because English cricket is in a mess and because the group of senior players who went to South Africa have been disqualified, young players have been thrust into Test matches far too early. It is not their fault. The organization which has carried on in the same old way for so long is badly at fault and must take the blame for the lack of forward planning.

I retired with a very impressive Test record – 8,114 runs for an average of 47.72 – and I mention that not to boast but to make an important point. I did not play for Yorkshire until the age of twenty-one and had reached twenty-three before I gained my first Test cap. Hussain and Atherton were thrust forward at least a year too soon, maybe two. In the old days the selectors would have given them another season in county cricket before easing one or the other into a tour party as the batsman least likely to figure in the Tests, taking him along to gain experience and learn about cricket at the top. As it is, England has reaped the whirlwind of its short-sighted complacency over the last decade. Far too many players have been picked for just a few Tests and then dropped again, without being given a chance to establish themselves.*

Youngsters are being thrown in at the deep end because there is nothing left, no veneer of experience to cover the cracks in English cricket. They emerge from the second teams and the universities with inferior techniques, which are just about adequate at county level but which are found wanting when put to the test by top-quality bowling. I have always argued that there are many county batsmen capable of putting together the odd good score in a Test match if they were to play long enough, but the best batsmen produce runs consistently in all conditions and against even the best bowlers. I have heard it argued that Sunil Gavaskar's record as the world's leading Test match run-maker reflects to a large extent preferential treatment from Indian umpires, but the 'little master' is credited with six Test centuries in the West Indies, including 220 at Port of Spain, and his runs came so regularly that his outstanding talent cannot seriously be questioned.

During all the coaching sessions with England I made extensive use of video equipment, filming each player. This enabled us to talk things through together afterwards and individuals could take home film of themselves to study. It is sometimes difficult for a batsman to accept that he has the fault you are pointing out, but when he sees the tape the impact is enormous.

Video is a very useful aid that has great potential for sportsmen. Entirely by chance, it helped to focus on another crippling limitation in England's approach to Test cricket. There is only one sensible place to position the video camera

* Jonathan Agnew: three Tests, 1984–5; Mark Benson: one, 1986; Alan Butcher: one, 1979; Roland Butcher: three, 1980; John Childs: two, 1988; Tim Curtis: two, 1988; Neil Fairbrother: four, 1987; Ian Greig: two, 1982; Alan Igglesden: one, 1989; David Lawrence: one, 1988; Andy Lloyd: one, 1984; Matthew Maynard: one, 1988; Paul Parker: one, 1981; Tony Pigott: one, 1983; Neil Radford: three, 1986–7; Arnie Sidebottom: one, 1985; Wilf Slack: three, 1985–6; David Smith: two, 1985; Les Taylor: two, 1985; Paul Terry: two, 1984.

and that is directly over the stumps at the bowler's end. At one stage during the coaching I was asked to move it to one side so the seamers could get in close to the stumps and I objected because the film is of no use if shot from an angle. 'These sessions are for bowlers as well as batsmen,' said Les Lenham, the National Cricket Association coach, revealing his own lack of knowledge about conditions overseas. Certainly it is helpful for bowlers to operate from close to the stumps in England, where the line to bowl is at the stumps because the ball seams around. In the West Indies, however, the ball behaves much more predictably, with less movement, and the batsmen murder anything down the line of wicket-to-wicket, whipping it through the leg side with heart-breaking assurance. To counter this, the bowler has to direct his attack at or slightly outside the off stump – giving it one extra stump in terms of width – so there is no point in starting the delivery from close in. Fortunately, I know that Geoff Arnold, the former Surrey and England paceman, passed on this important bit of information to the bowlers. Such a little incident, which might seem trivial in itself, shows how much there is to Test cricket that is a mystery to anyone who has not experienced it over a long period. There are so many things you cannot learn from a book.

This is why the Test and County Cricket Board have to take steps as a matter of extreme urgency to establish a panel of experts. During the time I spent coaching England, the opinions I had formed over several years were reinforced – mainly that on the whole ordinary county cricketers are not equipped to coach at the highest level. They simply do not have the right background. The kind of people I would like to see becoming involved in a long-term programme, starting with fourteen- and fifteen-year-olds, are, in addition to myself, Geoff Arnold, John Snow, Fred Titmus, Ray Illingworth, Norman Gifford, Derek Underwood, Alan Knott and Bob Taylor. We would form a group of top-class cricketers covering every aspect of the game:

batting, fast and fast-medium bowling, right- and left-arm spin bowling and wicketkeeping. The present generation of leading county players are technically so limited and so short of expertise that the strands of knowledge that held the first-class game together have been broken. In a few years there will be no-one left to tackle coaching on a master-class basis, because the former players who have so much to offer now will be too old to be bothered.

At the moment, England does not do enough with boys of above-average ability. Graham Saville, the former Essex batsman, coaches and is responsible for selecting the under-nineteens; and, in conjunction with the English Schools' Cricket Association, David Lloyd is becoming involved with those under fourteen and under fifteen. I would like to see the Test and County Cricket Board authorities setting up a national structure with four age-groups – under fifteen, under seventeen, under nineteen and under twenty-one. The cream of England's youngsters could then have high-quality coaching sessions during winter weekends, Easter holidays, summer holidays and at Christmas, in the course of which faults could be spotted early and eliminated.

It is easier to put schoolboys on the right road because being young they are naturally receptive to change, whereas the weaknesses of players over twenty tend to be ingrained. You cannot really start too early to teach a batsman mental discipline, the selection of strokes, how to play the turning ball, how to think his way through a situation and how to use his head and concentrate. Each group should have a full-time team-manager who could listen to what the experts were saying, put their ideas into practice and create a dossier with the help of notes and video film on each player. In that way the boys could work on various aspects of their game throughout the year, gradually developing as they move forward. Such a scheme would also ensure continuity, and would allow late developers to be introduced into the appropriate age-group. Obviously only the best prospects would be invited to join such a scheme, to ensure they received as much individual advice as possible. I could deal with the batsmen. I could not give any technical help to the bowlers, although as a batsman I could tell them where I would like them to bowl and what kind of bowling would cause me most problems. I was able, for example, to convince Devon Malcolm that a bouncer missing a batsman by a couple of feet is a waste of effort. The ball has to be aimed at him so that he has to respond, to take some positive, hasty action. 'Now I want you to bowl bouncers in the nets,' I told him, 'and make them count.' He did not like that. 'But I don't want to hit my team-mates, they're my friends,' he protested. 'Look,' I replied, 'they have all the necessary gear on – helmets, pads, chest pads, arm protector. What happens at their end is their problem. If you don't sharpen them up, how do you think they are going to cope with Ambrose or Walsh? Do you really think the West Indian pacemen are going to worry about hitting them?'

Someone like Arnold could deal with the seam bowlers while, perhaps, having the occasional word with the batsmen to give them an insight into the mind of the bowler. Chris Old, the former Yorkshire and England seamer, called in at Headingley during one of the England sessions. He had not been there at all long when Phil DeFreitas produced a couple of superb deliveries. 'Chris just showed me something about the way he held the ball,' DeFreitas explained, illustrating perfectly the value of specialist advice. County coaches are not doing the job properly. One man cannot know all about cricket, even if he understands the basics of batting, bowling and fielding. The more talented boys need the best possible advice from players who have performed well in Test cricket and gathered together a wealth of experience.

At the older end of the junior scale, an exchange system should be set up with Australia, New Zealand, West Indies, India and Pakistan, enabling young players to experience just how much pitches and general conditions vary abroad. If every English county agreed to look after two overseas boys the project would be very worthwhile. The Test and County Cricket Board, which is really all the counties, could decide which youngsters to send from their squads and everyone would benefit. Imagine how easily Yorkshire could counter the scurrilous accusations of racism that have been heaped on their heads by taking, say, an Indian and Pakistani teenager on to their staff, if only to figure in the second team or club and ground matches while practising with the first team and playing in the local leagues.

The counties themselves should also be encouraged to improve their coaching facilities. Northamptonshire enterprisingly recruited Australian ace Dennis Lillee, much to the delight of their bowlers, but for the most part county cricketers are left to their own devices once they reach first-team standard, and if anything goes wrong they are very much out on their own. How does Whitaker put something right at Leicestershire, where that very fine bowler Ken Higgs is coach? With no disrespect to Higgs, one of my old room-mates from the tours, he does not understand batting. I have spotted flaws in Whitaker's technique that could have and should have been corrected years ago, when he first joined the county. Surely it would pay the counties to put £10,000 each into a pool to cover the costs of establishing an expert coaching-panel? That figure is a drop in the ocean compared with their share of the Test match profits, which have reached some £4,500,000.

When Micky Stewart approached me and asked if I would help with the England coaching, money was never mentioned. I agreed because I was happy to do what I could to boost our chances during the winter, but at the end of a session he told me that there was a fee of £100 per day. 'Don't be insulted,' he pleaded. Well, I was insulted. It is not that I need the money; there is a principle at stake, for if things are done on the cheap they have no value. If you go to see a specialist in the medical field it will cost you at least £50 for quarter of an hour's consultation.

England's attitude reminds me of a story I was told as a boy. It concerns a man whose car broke down. Being unable to start it again himself, he sent for the mechanic from the local garage, who had a quick look inside the engine, then took out a large hammer, struck some part a sharp blow and said 'It's fine now. That'll be twenty-five pounds.' 'But it didn't take you five minutes,' complained the car owner. 'I charge one pound for the use of the hammer and twenty-four pounds because I know exactly which spot to hit,' said the mechanic, holding out his hand.

Top Test cricketers possess knowledge that cannot be acquired anywhere else; so England has no choice. It should either go to them for help and value them properly, or struggle along in ignorance as best it can. I honestly think that people like Underwood, Knott and Illingworth must be worth at least £500 a day, particularly as cricket's financial security is dependent on our national side competing successfully once more. If the counties cannot raise the money, or do not want to, then they should go out and get some sponsorship. In the long run, if the counties pay poor money for coaching they will get a poor end-product.

Golfers have coaches at every tournament and I am not talking about the also-rans scrambling for a few pounds well down the field. The most successful players in the world all team up with someone they trust, turning to them on a regular basis, and they make it worth the coaches' while to be available. Bob Torrance and David Leadbetter, two of the best-known and respected teaching professionals, are always present at tournaments. Torrance gets a retainer plus five per cent of the earnings of all the golfers on his class list. He is with them when they warm up before a tournament. He makes sure that their swing is nicely in the groove and that they are hitting the ball accurately, paying careful attention to their individual problems. Similarly in tennis, Ivan Lendl is right up at the top of the tree, but he still has Tony Roche constantly on hand to act as his mentor.

Although so much less money is available for cricket than for golf or tennis, there is no reason why its legislators should not adopt specialist coaching, although to do this the counties would have to sweep away their stubborn resistance to change. Cricketers are accustomed to drifting through the summer enjoying a bit of success one day and failing the next, which is why, I suppose, I stood out and became a loner. I could not stand failing, but a lot of players are content to write it off as bad luck.

Steve Oldham, Yorkshire's assistant coach before being prompted to the role of cricket manager, ran out of patience with Ashley Metcalfe in the summer of 1989 as the opener surrendered his wicket in match after match. Although not a batsman, Oldham felt he had to say something, mentioning a few thoughts about balance and the way Metcalfe was batting. In mid-sentence he was stopped by county coach Doug Padgett, who said: 'Leave him alone. He's a flair player. He comes and goes.' So many English cricketers have slipped into the same idiotic thinking. Technique is vital to success at Test Match level and faults have to be ironed out and kept to a minimum. The top players are forever working to perfect and finely tune their game.

Raising standards depends on county coaches being tough. There is no point in any coach wanting to be too friendly and relaxed or being too concerned about hurting people's feelings. When I am coaching or helping a player I tell him the truth and if it is unpalatable that is too bad. For example, I took the opportunity to watch the highly promising Middlesex batsman Mark Ramprakash during the 1989 county championship fixture with Yorkshire at Headingley. I had given him the Man of the Match award in the 1988 NatWest Trophy Final at Lord's for a well-organized 56, which proved decisive as Middlesex beat Worcestershire by three wickets in a low-scoring contest. As things turned out, I picked a very good day to follow up this contact and measure his progress, for Ramprakash completed his maiden first-class century and naturally received congratulations from his team-mates at lunch-time. I happened to be on the players' balcony talking to Mike Gatting when Ramprakash came to the dressing-room door. Mike asked me to have a word with him. 'Well played,' I said, 'but you were very lucky to finish with a century.' The understandable look of self-satisfaction faded from his face. 'I watched you very carefully, and you played a very poor shot on seventy-seven, a stroke that was totally wrong for the length of the ball.' It did not surprise me when Ramprakash offered an immediate explanation. 'There was only one slip, so I thought that if I got an edge it would fly safe ninety times out of a hundred,' he argued. I could have let it pass, and perhaps a lot of senior batsmen would have taken that easy option. Instead, I shook him. 'That is a stupid way to play. You've done all the hard work to get established and put yourself in control of the situation, yet you're ready to throw it away by taking an unnecessary risk.'

I also pressed the point that Ramprakash had lost his nerve a bit in the 90s and literally thrown his bat at the ball. 'Once they get in, great batsmen do not give the bowler any chance at all. They go on and on to make big hundreds,' I insisted. Overall, Ramprakash probably felt I had been very harsh and no doubt he wished I had not been there, but Gatting made a point of thanking me. 'I hope he listens to you,' he said. The point, of course, is that my advice was sound, based on hard-won experience, and I would have been doing a potential England cricketer a disservice if I had not told him the truth.

Literally hundreds of Yorkshire boys feared coach Arthur Mitchell. He ruled the Yorkshire nets with a rod of iron, and many a lad went home on a dark winter's night in tears after a roasting from 'Ticker'. I can never remember Mitchell uttering one word of praise, although many of us turned up time after time determined to impress. You were really lucky if he restricted himself to: 'Not too bad, but keep that left elbow up.' Mitchell, wearing his Yorkshire sweater with a county cap pulled low over his forehead, always stood behind the bowler's stumps watching everything like a hawk. Brian Close was so annoyed by his sharp-tongued criticism that he used to drive the ball as hard as he could straight back down the wicket in the hope, I am sure, of hitting Mitchell, or at least making him jump out of the way. Mitchell never budged and never softened, however. Not even the best really satisfied him. He wanted more and more for Yorkshire.

When I had become captain of Yorkshire and we were equals if not exactly friends, I told Mitchell: 'You were a bastard when I was a kid, Arthur. You were hard on us.' His expression never changed. 'Aye, well, my job was to turn out good Yorkshire cricketers. I had no time for weaklings and my way of doing things paid off.' A few Arthur Mitchells in the England coaching system might pay off, too. Mitchell worked on the principle that if you could survive rough treatment at his hands you could survive when the going got difficult in the middle. I wanted to play for Yorkshire so badly that his aggressive attitude only made me more determined to make the grade and, having done that, I raised the level of my ambition towards securing an England place. Many boys dream of playing for their country but comparatively few are ready to make the supreme sacrifices necessary to turn hope into reality. They like the idea without relishing all the hard work and application. My desire to win Test caps was so intense that it filled my life and my dedication turned me into a social outcast at times. A world that admires a painter or musician who dedicates himself to his art too readily sneers at a single-minded sportsman.

In avoiding the pint-swilling, back-slapping sessions in the bar I found myself regarded as a loner, even by leading officials who ought to have been pleased that I cared so much. Cocktail parties did not appeal to me but I attended them out of a sense of duty as a junior in the England ranks. When I was older and more sure of myself I put practice first and arrived at the social functions only when I could spare the time.

An anecdote from early in my Test career illustrates how keen I was to play for England. I was very ill in Ceylon on the way to Australia in 1965, and was confined to hospital while Eric Russell, from Middlesex, scored some runs in the state games. He broke his thumb, however, so although I had been out of action for six weeks Mike Smith, the captain, rushed me into the first Test. Still not really well and badly out of touch, I got through on 'automatic pilot', completing two half-centuries, and thought I was certain to keep my place, particularly as I went on to make some more runs up country. To my horror, however, when the second Test came around they dropped me to create room for Russell, now fit again, and I could not hide my anger and dismay. Billy Griffith, the manager, broke the bad news, adding that I was in the thirteen because Higgs had been taken ill. If he did not recover I would play, not just as a batsman but to supplement the bowling. I did not say a word. I could not trust myself to speak for a while, but when Griffith tried to smooth things over and imply that it was not the end of the world I exploded. 'Don't let Russell near me,' I shouted, 'or I'll push him down the stairs!' I did not really mean Russell any harm but the remark merely revealed, in the heat of the moment, how bitterly disappointed I was and how much playing meant to me. Yet it was taken out of that emotional context and repeated to highlight my lack of team-spirit. Actually, on the day of the Test Higgs woke up feeling groggy and I persuaded him to report sick. 'You'll never get through in this heat – it'll kill you!' I told him, so while he recuperated I played.

I realize that few players want to succeed as much as I did, so the rewards for those who do climb the mountains should be much greater. Payments increased substantially after Australian Kerry Packer rocked the establishment by setting up his alternative cricket circus, but there is room for further improvement. The Test and County Cricket

Board makes huge profits from the home Test series and it would pay the counties to give a bigger slice of the cake to those who represent their country. The more successful the England side, the bigger the surplus is likely to be each year. At the same time, those bigger match fees should have to be earned. A number of stars seem to believe they have a divine right to selection, whatever their form, and I suspect that the decision to omit David Gower from the tour to the West Indies was designed to shake him up a little. Mike Brearley, as captain, did much to create the club atmosphere in the England dressing-room, which is all right in one sense as it encourages unity. On the other hand, nobody should be allowed to take his place for granted. I never did, except, perhaps, if I had scored a century. Sir Alf Ramsey, in brilliantly masterminding England's triumph in the 1966 soccer World Cup, kept his squad on their toes. Departing home after one international, Gordon Banks, acclaimed as the best goalkeeper in the world, said casually: 'So long, see you next match.' 'Will you?' queried Ramsey, leaving Banks in no doubt that his team place wasn't automatically guaranteed.

Nothing can be taken for granted in sport, as England's experiences in the West Indies demonstrated. After all that hard work in their preparation for the tour, the players exceeded every expectation, including their own, by winning the first Test and coming agonizingly close to success in the third, following a complete wash-out of the second. They then fell away and eventually lost the series because, under increasing pressure, the batsmen reverted to bad habits.

Those in charge of the team forgot that coaching has to be ongoing, a continuous process of learning and development. Before the tour Gooch and Stewart took the sensible step and asked me if I would help out from time to time. Without hesitation, I agreed. They even went so far as to clear things with Sky Television, who had first claim on my time. Sadly, although I spoke to both Gooch and

Stewart many times in the Caribbean, they never asked me to coach during the net sessions. I feel that this was a serious mistake, because there was so much I could have contributed. Indeed, I have to admit to a sense of real frustration as I watched Stewart, Bailey and Hussain make the very mistakes I had corrected at Headingley and Lilleshall. I remain convinced that England had gone a long way down the right road in their build-up to the series. But the team needed both a batting and a bowling coach on the tour itself, especially in the two days before each Test.

It might be that some people in the Test and County Cricket Board hierarchy were wary of using me because of my connection with Sky Television and *The Sun* newspaper, but the position had been the same when I worked with the players before the tour. There was no trouble then, and so far as I was concerned there would not have been any in the West Indies.

If the Test and County Cricket Board really wants to boost the team's prospects it should find the money to provide specialist coaching on a regular basis.

It all boils down to a question of priorities. Giving England the best chance of success means putting the emphasis on coaching and continuity.

2

The best
finishing-school
in the world

The English county championship used to be the best
finishing-school in the world, a marvellously broad-based
competition in which those fortunate enough to take part
could hone their skills to a fine edge. Consistently high
standards of performance were demanded, but while winning was obviously important committees and captains put
great stress on the right sort of attitude and behaviour. The
game was crammed with character and quality, the younger
element being kept in their place and tutored by the senior
professionals whose authority, under the captain, was never
challenged.

Sadly, that is no longer true. The most searching test of
ability, the three-day game, has been pushed into the background and squeezed into a variety of unsuitable shapes
to accommodate one-day cricket. Those in authority have
sacrificed quality in pursuit of increased revenue. Money,
I accept, is important, but there has to be a sensible balance
between financial considerations and the need to preserve
all that is best on the cricket-field. In the early 1960s
Yorkshire played at least 114 days of first-class cricket,

a figure that had shrunk to an inadequate seventy-two by 1989. Following a lemming-like course towards disaster, the supporters of a four-day championship programme, with each county meeting all the others once, are content to cut another eight days out of the season, supposedly to improve the prospects of the Test team. So many silly ideas emerge from Lord's that this latest foolishness should come as no surprise. Four-day cricket will be a mistake, as the South Africans discovered. They played their domestic competition over four days for long enough to recognize the weaknesses, so they successfully cut down to three. The public becomes bored with protracted matches, the players fritter away the extra time and the fixture schedule gets hopelessly complicated.

Too many games have finished early – one between Yorkshire and Nottinghamshire at Headingley, occupying no more than nine hours – and those that were stretched across the full course generally drifted along at far too leisurely a pace. Yorkshire captain Phil Carrick summed up the feeling in most dressing-rooms when, as the Test and County Cricket Board introduced a mix of three- and four-day fixtures in 1988, he said: 'It will be nice to win the toss and sit back for a couple of days knowing that there will not be a decision to make about a declaration.' The main plank in the four-day platform is the theory that it will enable emerging batsmen and bowlers to develop on the county circuit free from the pressures of the clock. According to the propaganda the batsmen will be able to build an innings and the bowlers will have to work for their wickets, and the quality of the graduates to the England ranks will rise accordingly. Nothing could be further from the truth. Extra time actually allows the poorer batsmen to graft out bigger scores, while the fielding side, rarely needing to take wickets in a hurry, sits back and waits for its turn at the crease. As anyone who has played in a successful county championship side will confirm, the time factor is an important element in separating the most accomplished players from the merely competent. The real weakness in English cricket is that the Test and County Cricket Board seldom addresses the basic problems. For instance, a lot of nonsense has been talked about the balls used at first-class level.

We even reached the point at which captains David Gower and Allan Border agreed to toss up for the choice of which ball to use during the England–Australia series of 1989, as it was claimed one make favoured seam bowlers more than the alternative. To my mind, there was nothing wrong with the type of ball used throughout my twenty-five-year career. However, it has become fashionable to complain about the shape of the ball during a match and umpires are constantly being pestered about this by the fielding side. Indeed, it could be regarded as a modern tactic. Some balls do swing more than others for no obvious reason, so bowlers are inclined to try to change one that is not moving about. Before the start of an innings the fielding team can choose whichever ball it prefers from a batch of three, and I firmly believe they should have to make do with what they get unless there is a very serious flaw in the manufacture. Yorkshire's lowest first-class total, of twenty-three against Hampshire at Middlesbrough in 1965, came at a time when Brian Close, as captain, was using a batch of balls specifically requested to have bigger-than-average seams and an extra row of stitching, in an attempt to win more matches. He reckoned that as we had an outstanding bowling attack in Trueman, Nicholson, Illingworth and Wilson, Yorkshire would profit from ensuring that the advantage lay with the bowlers. Things backfired with a vengeance at Acklam Park. The batsmen had little or no chance as the ball moved about alarmingly. I got nought in the first innings, at the end of which Yorkshire surrendered a lead of four. Never having endured the indignity of a pair, I worked out a plan to at least get off the mark when facing Derek Shackleton at the second attempt. He operated with computerized accuracy, always keeping a fairly full length and never giving anything away. After taking my guard, I advanced about a yard down the pitch while Shackleton marched back to his mark, so that the first ball was turned into a half-volley which I gratefully despatched through the covers for four. That trick succeeded only once and, after squirting an inside edge for one more, I departed lbw to Butch White, who finished with 6–10, figures which convinced me that it does not pay to meddle with the equipment.

Pitches are another topical issue, largely because the Test and County Cricket Board is obsessed with uniformity. The Board issued a directive which required groundsmen to put the emphasis on pace and bounce, with the Oval generally being held up as an ideal. No-one, unfortunately, appreciated that what suited Surrey's headquarters might well be harmful on another ground, and things got worse rather than better. There is, in fact, no universal panacea. A variety of playing surfaces is the natural course of things, with the weather and soil in Sheffield, for instance, being totally different from the weather and soil in Canterbury or Worcester. Some strips usually favour batsmen, while bowlers look forward to bowling on others with a justifiable sense of anticipation. Much of the attraction of the championship has its roots in the different conditions, which ensure that players become adaptable. Bowlers and batsmen have to develop all-round skills as they face and master a variety of problems. The end-product is or should be a succession of players with sound techniques who are prepared for every occasion. Nothing really takes them by surprise.

The main problem today is the variable bounce, which can make the best batsman in the world look second-rate. Those of us who got to the top learned to cope with lateral movement and our reputations were built on the ability to make late adjustments, coupled with the judgement which enabled us to leave alone a lot of dangerous deliveries as they swung or seamed away late. But no batsman can operate with any degree of confidence if he cannot play right forward safely. Once he becomes worried about the ball lifting unpredictably he is lost, and his innings involves an unacceptable degree of chance. It is therefore essential that groundsmen are encouraged to get back to basics, with even bounce as the main objective. Otherwise, they should be left alone to produce the type of pitch that is best suited to local conditions.

It is also a mistake to cover the pitches whenever it rains. This has been a thorny topic of debate for many years and admittedly uncovered pitches, affected by rain, can give one side an overwhelming advantage. But they also teach batsmen to play properly and add spice to a match by introducing an unknown factor, an element of the unpredictable which gives crowds something to look forward to. On the true, fast pitches that are supposedly the ideal, batsmen can whack the ball away without getting into the correct position, creating the illusion that they are better than they are. I began on uncovered pitches which, after getting wet, demanded the highest level of skill and application, as well as the ability to improvise. It was impossible to survive by throwing the bat at the ball because, even with a lot of good fortune, the player lacking in technique would get only a dozen or so runs before being dismissed. He had little or no chance slogging. Uncovered pitches got much slower after rain, allowing the ball to turn and move off the seam. A vociferous group of alleged experts maintain that they prevented young batsmen developing. Nonsense. What the more testing conditions did was to increase the pressure on batsmen, because on a slow pitch the contact between bat and ball had to be absolutely perfect. There were many magnificent bowlers who could exploit the slow, turning pitch and as a batsman you had to wait for the ball, timing your response exactly. If, for example, you were trying to work the off-spinner towards mid-wicket and played too soon you got a leading edge and the ball lobbed gently into the air. It is a kind of modern disease that batsmen on covered pitches play so much across the line, a basic problem which would soon be cured if the covers were taken off once a match started.

Facing a decent left-arm spinner on a slow pitch was a challenge. Even when the ball was not jumping, the batsman could not afford to look to score on the on side. He had to play straight or with the spin, delaying his stroke until the last possible split-second to ensure he brought the full face of the bat into play. His defensive technique had to be of the highest quality. He had to remain very watchful, allowing the ball to come on to him so that he could play with the spin and ride it, using 'soft hands' to eliminate the risk of giving a catch. It was essential to get everything right to drop the ball down dead.

The golfer competing on a wet course requires the same degree of skill when using an iron. If he strikes the merest fraction too far behind the ball, the soggy turf will get between club and ball and kill the power, taking yards off the shot. This is why the leading golfers practise in sand with long irons. They know it is vital to strike the ball perfectly to achieve a satisfactory length. Equally, the batsman with a poor technique cannot hope to rely on sheer power on a slow pitch, because the ball will either balloon in the air or the bat will complete the swing too soon and he will be bowled 'through the gate'. The best players, those able to wait and play each delivery on its merits, always made runs, and there was a great beauty and fascination in the way that a classical batsman like Len Hutton or Dennis Compton met such a challenge. They approached an innings differently, with Compton being unorthodox, ready to improvise, and Hutton elegantly embellishing the more tried-and-tested methods, but they both had the ingrained ability to overcome any difficulty. In coping with so many different surfaces batsmen found it necessary to adapt mentally, applying the mind as well as the body.

A check through the 1960s record books would reveal that when Yorkshire batted on a rain-affected pitch, Geoff

Boycott, Doug Padgett and Ray Illingworth regularly scored more runs than the rest of the side. We were all very correct players and Illingworth was a much better technician than the flashy Bryan Stott, unpredictable Ken Taylor or Phil Sharpe, who had only a small stride forward and who did not bend his left knee enough. Standing correctly sideways on, Illingworth always got right back or right forward and played within his limitations, with a cool head and a keen eye to the situation. Many of his more substantial contributions to Yorkshire's cause with the bat came with the innings subsiding alarmingly and he was able to turn things round because he employed such a correct technique. The lessons he absorbed on uncovered pitches served him in good stead when, as England's off-spinner captain in his late thirties, he still made runs in Test cricket.

Uncovered pitches were also splendid from the paying public's point of view. I have taken part in some wonderful sessions, with the ball moving about and spectators not daring to look away for a second in case they missed something. On those occasions there would be an audible sigh of relief when the luncheon or tea interval arrived, and you could almost feel the whole ground relax as the tension eased. Today, championship cricket is cloaked in drab uniformity and the brief experiment with a compromise allowing partial covering in 1987 did nothing more than reveal how little they understand at Lord's.

The regulations allowed for the playing surface to be protected overnight but not during the hours of play, and the bowlers' run-ups could be covered whenever the weather interfered with play. It is hard to imagine a more muddled, half-hearted attempt to re-introduce the natural element of the weather into the game, and, predictably, hardly anyone experienced playing a spinner on a drying strip. The only rain to get on to the pitch had to fall during the hours of play, which meant that long delays ensued when no play was possible. Once the match started again the fast bowlers roared up to threaten life and limb, with the ball leaping at the batsmen's heads. Overnight rain does not necessarily prevent play, although it may delay the start, and exposed run-ups force the fielding side to use the slow bowlers because it becomes too slippery for the pacemen. A good contest then takes place between the batsmen and the spinners. Unfortunately, there is today a tendency to make the weather a good reason for not playing at all. To become self-financing, the championship must be attractively packaged and presented. The show must go on whenever it is possible. Odd wet patches, however disconcerting to the fielding side, should never be allowed to keep the players in the dressing-room, and very firm official instructions should be issued to help umpires handle the hazards of rain and bad light. There is no doubt that the various one-day competitions continue in conditions that would be unacceptable in the championship, yet the same players and umpires are involved. League clubs also cheerfully play when first-class cricketers would not. Luck should play some part in the game.

Far too many excuses are made for England's short-comings, the presence of overseas players being one of the most popular. A plausible argument along these lines could have been put forward in the 1970s, but I see nothing to worry about now when all counties are limited to one overseas player. An overseas player is taking the place of the weakest member of a team and logically he has a lot more to offer. Obviously there have been exceptions, but as a general rule an established overseas Test star can help younger colleagues to improve, while acting as a crowd-puller and a focal point for sponsorship. In any case, I suspect that the supply is drying up, with fewer outstanding figures striding across the world stage. Even the highly successful Australians of 1989 were a well-organized collective unit rather than a galaxy of brilliant individuals. The doubters should consider carefully how much players such as Richards, Marshall, Rice or Hadlee have contributed to the English game in return for their generous salaries. I suggest

31

the balance of evidence confirms that these world-class professionals, who stand shoulder-to-shoulder with the greatest talents of all time, have given far more than they have taken. I would go further and insist that it is entirely the fault of the younger cricketers if they have not derived greater benefit from the presence on the circuit of such superb role-models. The truth is that the whole structure of English cricket needs close examination, starting with the coaching system and the management of boys coming into the game, many of whom are easily satisfied with limited horizons and a comfortable life.

Easy options and quick rewards are readily available. The players' parking area at the average county ground is packed with expensive motor cars, some emblazoned with names hardly anyone has heard of, followed by the words 'county cricketer', which is almost an offence under the Trades Descriptions Act. I waited until I played for England before purchasing my first car. Presumably because they assume I have a lot of influence, youngsters sometimes seek my help in securing their first sponsored car. 'I'll see what I can do,' I tell them and then ask: 'What can I tell the sponsor you will do for him in return?', a question which invariably draws a blank look. 'Well, nothing really, I just want a car,' is the standard response.

It is the same with their approach to cricket itself. I *loved* batting and I do not use the word lightly. I didn't just like batting, I loved it, so everything else in life had to come second. The modern generation, I suspect, are more interested in the rewards to be had from the game. I earned a reputation for being fanatical about practice and my personal form, although many of the stories grew with the telling. I will be the first to admit that I hated getting out and I did sit quietly in a corner of the dressing-room on my return to the pavilion. Usually I was angry with myself, but I never threw down my bat, and I reckoned that the only way to get rid of the frustration was to consider every aspect of my dismissal in an attempt to ensure that I cut down the margin for error in future. I analyzed every delivery that claimed my wicket, searching for ways to strengthen my defence, and if that made me unpopular, then tough luck.

One day in the summer of 1989 Norman Shuttleworth, the chairman of Leeds Cricket, Football and Athletic Club, which owns Headingley, looked out over an almost-deserted ground and said: 'Over so many years I've come up here on company business and must have seen Boycott in the nets for thousands of hours. There were days when I saw him in the morning, in the afternoon and again in the evening, batting and batting for as long as he could persuade anyone to bowl at him. Now the nets are often empty.' His remarks were not so much praise for my dedication, which came as second nature to me, but more a comment on modern attitudes. Some youngsters are bone idle and will not train or practise unless given a directive. Once the discipline of the early season has gone, fit and lean young men let things slide, and often resemble chocolate bobbies by the end of June. I wonder what county coaches think they are doing in turning a blind eye to such laziness. It is appalling when players report back from the winter break badly out of condition, yet many of those in charge of cricket in counties all over the country shrug their shoulders and say: 'There's not much I can do, we don't pay them in winter. They can do what they like.' That may be true according to the letter of the law, but if those who turned up unprepared for serious practice were left out of the first team in the early weeks or made to put in extra hours of pre-season training, things would soon improve. There are batsmen in county cricket, some with England caps, parading dreadfully flawed techniques and oblivious to criticism. The virtues of the past are dismissed as 'old fashioned'. How would getting rid of overseas players or stretching the championship over four days make them better cricketers? How would it raise their standards or make them less complacent?

It is a very old adage that a chain is as strong as its weakest link and the quality of county cricket is clearly related to the quality of league cricket, which in my opinion has deteriorated alarmingly. It amazed me to find on the occasions when I appeared with Castleford in the Yorkshire League that I was one of the best bowlers in the team. I found it easy to bowl accurately and economically, so they tried to make a lot of use of my tidy medium-pace. I rationed myself to a few overs, however, as I did not want to put a strain on my back and, in any case, Castleford's aim should have been to make their regular bowlers more effective. Using me to get them off the hook on an occasional basis did not help the side to improve. Many admirable and devoted people with good league credentials put a lot of time and effort into coaching at centres of excellence and among juniors at club level, but they can go only so far because they lack experience of the first-class game. To improve the standard of league cricketers good habits have to be instilled at an early age. It would pay counties to send coaches around the leagues to teach the teachers. Experienced county professionals could raise the standards during the winter months and everyone would benefit. The county cricketers would have a good job, the local league coaches would learn more about the game, and the boys in schools and clubs would get better advice. The presence of a well-known sportsman at coaching sessions might also fire the enthusiasm of the youngsters.   In the end, though, a great deal depends on the type of cricket played on the first-class circuit, so the only way forward is to recreate a sensible championship. There is no doubt that the major competition has been downgraded by too much limited-overs cricket which chops up the season and prevents the development of a steady rhythm. Ironically, it is the one-day version of the game that attracts much of the television and newspaper coverage. A whole generation has grown up convinced that the Sunday League, the Benson and Hedges Cup and the NatWest Trophy are what really matter, their views being conditioned by the fact that counties demand to select from full-strength squads for the knockout ties, while the Sunday afternoon slog regularly attracts the television cameras. It is against this background that far too many players have come to regard the championship as a chore, a boring routine to fill in the time between more important engagements. What was once a fascinating battle for supremacy has slowly but surely turned into two days of casual stalemate followed by a hectic last afternoon declaration run-chase. This is no sort of preparation for Test cricket and even this poor imitation of the real thing is strictly rationed for members of the England side. For years the system has denied our leading performers serious match practice between Tests and many players have been regularly left without any cricket for spells in July and August. A quick glance through the fixtures for 1989 reveals the difficulties experienced by, for example, Graham Gooch, as he wrestled with a failing technique, gathering self-doubt, and veteran seamer Terry Alderman in the series with Australia.

After the one-day internationals, which kept him out of two three-day games with Essex, Gooch did not have a championship match before the first Test. Between the first and second Tests he appeared with Essex against Leicestershire and before moving on to the third Test he squeezed in a championship engagement with Sussex. There was the big bonus of six days' serious cricket leading up to the fourth Test, but only one championship match as a prelude to the fifth and final Test. The outcome of all this was that only fifteen days' championship cricket was available to England's key batsman throughout the whole of the international programme. When he desperately needed to spend a lot of time in the middle working things out in his mind, Gooch found himself being hurried along by the dictates of the Benson and Hedges Cup, NatWest Trophy or Sunday League regulations. The case for a complete reorganization is overwhelming and I would start by doing away with the Sunday League, which is a nuisance and is rapidly losing popularity as attendances decline. The Benson and Hedges Cup, certainly in its present form, would have to go as well because it complicates fixtures, especially in the early weeks of the summer when players require proper cricket. The NatWest Trophy could profitably be retained and moved to late August and September after the Tests, to provide a suitably spectacular climax to the season. The Trophy covers five playing days and, with September often being a reasonably good month for weather, two to three weeks should be sufficient to complete the matches while reawakening interest in the affairs of counties out of the running in the championship race.

Unfortunately, the ill-considered four-day plan is by no means the only handicap weighing down the championship, which is dogged by a bonus points system too complicated for the casual observer to follow. Cutting away the dead wood is not in itself a complete answer, therefore. I envisage a vibrant championship that will capture the imagination of the public and the attention of the new television services jostling to cover worthwhile sporting occasions. The competition should be given a complete new image, firstly by increasing the programme to a minimum of twenty-eight matches, running from mid-May, which is soon enough to start, to September. To give the championship the prominence it deserves, fixtures could be spread over Saturday, Sunday and Monday, and Wednesday, Thursday and Friday, with extended hours of play up to 7.00p.m. or even 7.30p.m. to encourage people to watch on their way home from work. In placing the emphasis firmly on entertainment without making damaging concessions in terms of quality, I would introduce a simple method of speeding up play.

It is not asking too much to demand nineteen overs an hour from teams, so, working on the basis of a normal day starting at 11.00a.m. and finishing at 7.30p.m., it would be possible to have three sessions of two-and-a-half hours, each containing forty-seven overs, a total, assuming no interruptions, of one hundred and forty-one overs. To assist with the travelling arrangements, the third day could be reduced to two sessions involving ninety-four overs, with the option of an extra hour and nineteen extra overs for either side if they were in a position to force victory. Admittedly it is not always possible to play on into the evening in May and September, but there is nothing wrong in keeping the action going for as long as possible with 7.30p.m. as the target. Allowances would be made for rain or bad light on the basis of one over for every three minutes lost. The present Test and County Cricket Board system of fines for counties who average less than eighteen and a half overs an hour in each half of the season and overall does not work effectively because the players either make up lost ground in matches that have drifted into stalemate or they accept the penalties and hope to pay them out of their bonus money. I would ensure an even flow by insisting on the minimum forty-seven overs in each session, punishing a side falling behind the rate in two ways. At the interval the batting side would be awarded 10 runs, to be recorded as extras, for every over below the requirement. Additionally, the fielding side would have to complete the allocation in their own time. A shorter lunch or tea-break would not worry the batsmen unduly, but I can see the fielders being very unhappy.

A straightforward points allocation with rewards for winning and for a first-innings lead would remove any confusion and, with a genuine sense of urgency injected into the proceedings, counties would soon realize that they could not afford to amble along. By getting only a handful of overs behind the rate they would virtually forfeit any hope of winning as the extras mounted alarmingly, so it should become standard practice for all sides to include two spinners and use them. With a good product to promote, cricket would be in a strong position. Sky Television paid the West Indies Board far more than they had ever received for the right to screen the series against England in 1990 and a number of other television companies will be seeking ways of filling their schedules. Cricket could be ideally placed to fill the mid-week gaps if only the championship could be transformed. So far as limited overs cricket is concerned familiarity has clearly bred contempt among the spectators. But there would be scope for a one-day league on the Tuesday of each week, with sixty overs a side available to give it much more significance than the forty over hit-or-miss Sunday business.

Before a Test match, England players would miss these Tuesday one-day games in order to have two days to prepare themselves for the big game. I always hated having to dash from one end of the country to the other to represent England, the amount of travelling turning what was really an honour into something of a nightmare. Often it was so hectic that I hoped we would field first just so I could have a bit of time to prepare myself mentally. The Test and County Cricket Board tours committee insists on a two-day break before Tests overseas and the same thinking should apply at home. No doubt some counties would object to losing their top players on a Tuesday, but so much money comes from the Test profits these days that even self-interest dictates the necessity of giving England every opportunity to do well. For the first time in 1989, Yorkshire's share of the Test match account amounted to more than members' subscriptions, and that is a fact that cannot be ignored. To ensure any changes in the county set-up brought the expected dividends, a strict set of guidelines with far-reaching consequences would have to be vigorously enforced, not only by Lord's but also by the umpires, who have carried a heavy burden in controversial areas such as determining what is intimidatory bowling. They should be told officially to take charge and control matches, thus winning the respect of the players, who do try it on with the weaker officials. In my experience, the majority have been both fair and competent. Those who get to the top do so by force of character as well as by ability, commanding respect by sheer force of personality. My good friend Dickie Bird is among the best and although he gives the impression of being a bundle of nerves he is decisive and authoritative.

The Centenary Test at Lord's in 1980 turned out to be an anti-climax because of the weather and England never got in a position to win. I followed the instructions of captain Ian Botham in making sure we did not lose by scoring an unbeaten 128, frustrating the Australians in the process. Len Pascoe reacted by frequently pitching short. I was so wrapped up in building my innings that I did not fully appreciate Dickie's intervention, but I understand that it took very much the following course.

> *Bird*: 'That's enough, Len, keep the ball a lot further up.'
> *Pascoe*: 'I don't know what you mean, I'm not bowling short.'
> *Bird*: 'I think you are and I'm telling you to stop.'
> *Australian captain Greg Chappell, joining in the debate*: 'He's not bowling too short.'
> *Bird*: I've made my decision and I'm not asking for any other opinions.'

With that, he marched across to inform his colleague David Constant of the first warning, making it quite clear the argument was over. Finally, Pascoe conceded: 'All right, Dickie, you're the boss.' A weaker umpire than Dickie might easily have backed away from a potential confrontation, but that is not his style and he is respected throughout the world for invariably being both fair and firm. Ken Palmer, the former seamer, is another strong umpire. I stood almost mesmerized alongside him at Cheltenham in August 1979, when Mike Procter completed an lbw hat-trick against Yorkshire, remarkably the second of his incident-packed career. Richard Lumb, Bill Athey and John Hampshire were given out offering no discernible stroke to Procter, operating round the wicket, Palmer raising his finger for the third time in as many balls with the words: 'As God is my witness, that is out as well – and thank goodness it's the end of the over.'

The Test and County Cricket Board expects a lot from umpires, asking them to make a series of finely balanced judgements, yet their assessments of them are based on the reports of county captains who are not necessarily impartial when they put pen to paper. It is very easy for a captain, in the heat of the moment, to mark down an umpire on one important decision, ignoring the game as a whole. As captain of Yorkshire I made a point of regularly discussing the umpires with other members of the dressing-room because I appreciated that my views could be clouded by personal involvement. If I had been adjudged lbw, I would ask the non-striker what he thought and I also sought the opinions of my bowlers and the wicketkeeper, for they were the people in the best position to form an opinion on the umpires' performance. I am sure that many other captains have gone to great lengths to be fair and objective, but that is not the point. Umpires are likely to be very wary of the captains simply because they know they are marked by them. However honest and decent a captain might be, a grey area of uncertainty exists and references are made to 'a captain's decision', implying that the benefit of the doubt had been given to the man who sends in the report on the umpire.

It must surely be preferable, therefore, to employ a number of assessors and let them go quietly about the county circuit, making their own observations and talking to players and officials. Assessors could also hold confidential inquests with umpires behind closed doors, keeping everything low-key before reporting back to Lord's. Umpires, for their part, would not feel so isolated from the people deciding their futures and, therefore, their livelihoods. Of course, the cost has to be considered. The Test and County Cricket Board does not have a bottomless pocket, but quality and efficiency do not come cheap. This thought should be occupying the attentions of county committees all over the country, for cricket hardly holds out glittering career prospects. A comparative handful of outstanding players with that intangible star quality make a lot of money and will continue to do so, but the ordinary professionals exist in a different financial bracket.

A crop of ambitious, bright, fresh-faced boys representing Young England against Young New Zealand at Canterbury in August 1989 collectively subscribed to the view that county cricketers are not well paid. Actual hardship does not exist on the scale of the late nineteenth century when ex-cricketers were reduced to the most menial tasks in their declining years or were forced to rely on charity, but there is no long-term security. Players have to earn a living when they leave the game in their thirties or forties and few are comfortably placed unless they receive a benefit. Yorkshire at one time paid its capped players during winter and summer on a sliding scale, although no engagement covered more than one year which meant the poor professionals were vulnerable to injury or loss of form. They were at the mercy of the committee, too. One year the lucky Yorkshire players were called in turn to secretary John Nash's office to be informed that they would receive eight pounds in summer and six in winter. As they filed out they informed their colleagues of their good fortune, so it came as a nasty shock to Arthur Mitchell when he was told his wages would be eight pounds in summer and four pounds in winter. 'How can that be, Mr Nash?' he enquired. 'All the others are getting six pounds in winter.' 'The committee must think they are better players, I imagine,' said Nash. 'What, in winter?' exploded the irate Mitchell. Despite all the shortcomings, Mitchell and his contemporaries were better off than their successors, who are now paid from April to September. What they do for the other six months is up to them. Counties are missing a golden chance to exploit one of their most important assets for half of each year.

The awarding of contracts for a full year would create a willing workforce to coach and promote the county on a wide scale by linking it with the business world. Certainly the better-known cricketers in each county have at least a localized commercial value and each could be sponsored by a company during the summer in return for their services in the winter. For example, the Kent captain or the leading Warwickshire batsmen can stroll through doors firmly closed to an ordinary sales representative and there are many avenues to be explored by an imaginative administration. Indeed, county committees have a clear duty to stimulate their staff, for the majority are remote and indifferent and fail to get the best out of their players. Big business has discovered that the way to achieve efficiency and productivity is to keep the workers content, to acknowledge their contribution and to treat them as individuals.

Throughout all my troubles with Yorkshire I tried to play with the team's best interests at heart, but members of the committee dodged about in the background, looking for reasons to sack me, and causing the trouble they complained about in public. No-one directed their energies towards holding Yorkshire cricket together and I have heard enough dressing-room gossip to know that discontent is also rife in other clubs which does not make the headlines. After being made captain in 1971 I had to try to compensate for the limitations of the other batsmen and to guard against a whispering campaign by committee-men who should have been working for the good of Yorkshire cricket. Is it any wonder that Yorkshire continued to struggle and that some good youngsters with England potential failed to make the expected progress?

Free expression, taken for granted by every golfer and tennis player, who can pick and choose how and where they play, is denied to the cricketer, and that is something that those in charge of county clubs should think about very carefully. Who are the personalities capable of drawing the crowds today? They are few and far between. Yorkshire had a 'full house' crammed in behind locked gates for their Sunday League clash with Worcestershire at Scarborough in July 1989, the big attraction being Ian Botham, but he cannot go on for ever and there are few names coming forward to replace him. Graeme Hick, Worcestershire's Zimbabwean run-maker, is a wonderful batsman and people want to see him in action, but he is a rarity alongside much that is commonplace. Those of us who established ourselves as strong personalities were condemned as self-seekers and were accused of destroying team spirit. 'Boycott thinks he is bigger than the club,' my critics on the committee screamed in all those winters of discontent, but that was not true. The members who rose up to support me and eventually carry a vote of no confidence in the administration did not think so either. I happened to be the best player and the most famous personality in Yorkshire cricket, nothing more, and the club should have been keen to exploit my popularity instead of trying to destroy it by attaching sinister motives to everything I did. Instead of capitalizing on the fact that I became the first English batsman to average 100 in a season in 1971, most of the committee dismissed the achievement as an act of pure selfishness.

There is a widespread unease in official circles if the public elevates any player above his supposed station. This stifles individuality, kills personality and breeds middle-of-the-road players. In the early 1960s, as a starry-eyed newcomer to the circuit, I saw Gordon Barker of Essex put together a superb innings on a Sheffield pitch allowing Illingworth some turn. Not many did that and I could not understand why Barker was not playing for England. He quickly dispelled my illusions. 'I could get more runs,' he told me, 'but I settle for about thirteen hundred each season. If you get more one year the committee expects you to do it every time and if you don't it's looking to get rid of you. I can manage that, so I don't put myself under any unnecessary pressure.' That philosophy left me speechless. It contradicted everything I believe in.

In 1972, in an attempt to resolve one of my many contractual disputes with Yorkshire, who were resisting my request for £3,000 a year, I proposed that they pay me £1 per run in all competitions. This provoked a horrified response, yet the suggestion made sound economic sense for them and would have provided a tremendous incentive for me. Were I put in charge of any county I would certainly offer extra financial rewards, as did Lord Hawke when he laid the foundations upon which so much Yorkshire success was built. He had a book in which he awarded merit marks, which were translated into money at an annual gathering at his home. In that way those who put most in got most out.

There is a lot to be gained from a complete investigation into county cricket, with people who have played and watched the game over a long period being consulted. I cannot envisage anything better for the well-being of English cricket than a revival of the championship system of the 1950s and 1960s which produced so many truly great performers.

3

Poor p. r.

In my twenty-five years in the game nothing has changed so dramatically as the attitude of the media people. The press, blindly trampling across the boundaries of good taste, has seriously damaged cricket's public image over the past two decades, aided and abetted by the authorities at Lord's. Generations of journalists and players grew up together respecting an unwritten but readily recognized code of conduct which limited comments to events on the field. Once stumps had been drawn, relationships were maintained on an unofficial basis, with no attempt being made to pry into private lives. If a player overstepped the mark and subsequently failed to do either himself or his side justice, some mild, guarded reference might slip into one or two reports, and usually the offender took the warning and was more careful. The principal consideration was always the good of the game, and the extent to which cricket writers were prepared to go to serve sport's best interests can be gauged from their reaction to events at Leyton in 1925, when Percy Fender, the famous if slightly eccentric Surrey captain, and Johnny Douglas, of Essex, fell out.

Surrey batted first and made 431–8 declared, to which Essex replied with 333–7 by the close on Monday. Shortly before the scheduled starting-time on Tuesday, Fender discovered that all his Surrey professionals were missing, trapped in their charabanc in what must have been the forerunner of our modern traffic-jams. Only he and another amateur, Alfred Jeacocke, were available, but Douglas refused to hold up play, apparently insisting that he would claim the match if Surrey did not take the field. By all accounts only a handful of spectators were in the ground and they must have been amazed when the umpires marched out followed by only two Surrey men.

Eventually the Essex batsmen, C.J. Treglown and R.H. Sharp, who expressed a marked reluctance to continue the innings, took their place in the middle and quietly defended while Fender and Jeacocke got through four or five overs, directing their attack well wide of the stumps. The exact details remain a matter for conjecture, for the scorers recorded nothing in their books until the rest of the Surrey team reached the ground and the contest proceeded along more orthodox lines. The press obligingly drew a veil over the initial exchanges. Some reporters mentioned in passing that the Surrey charabanc had been delayed and the *Daily Mail* referred to Fender and Jeacocke waiting for their professional colleagues, but that was as far as it went. As a consequence, the bizarre incident passed almost unnoticed, although rumour grew up around it, notably in Essex. Fender and Douglas, spared the embarrassment of exposure to widespread gossip, emerged with their reputations intact, and cricket avoided unwelcome and unfavourable publicity.

All the same, I would not give whole-hearted support to similar action today. There is a danger in being overprotective and, while I sympathize with the sentiments of the journalists at Leyton, I am far from convinced that they were right. Another incident, deeply etched into the memories of the Yorkshire members, occurred at Northampton on 17 July, 1978, when John Hampshire and Colin Johnson scraped eleven runs from ten overs. Hampshire attempted only four scoring strokes from fifty-nine deliveries in what appeared to be some sort of protest. Two representatives of national newspapers had telephoned their stories on the earlier play and departed to the bar, but two writers from the local press, unhappy about what they had seen, pressed their enquiries. They filed highly critical pieces which fuelled the flames of another controversy and I honestly believe they took the correct course.

They felt that their first duty was to their employers, so they reported exactly what they had seen, added the statistics from the official score-books and interviewed me, Hampshire and Johnson, plus secretary Joe Lister and cricket committee member Billy Sutcliffe, who had both witnessed the closing stages of the Yorkshire innings. Hampshire, as the senior partner, could not escape the consequences of his actions and the Yorkshire public had a right to be informed of what had taken place.

As my career progressed, J. M. Kilburn of the *Yorkshire Post*, Bill Bowes of the *Yorkshire Evening Post*, Jim Swanton of the *Daily Telegraph* and John Arlott of the *Guardian*, maintained standards of tact and integrity, but I quickly discovered that the more popular daily newspapers were happy to make mischief. Somehow an unguarded word in the most casual conversation could be taken out of context and shaped into a story that commanded the most damning headlines.

I had hardly settled into the Yorkshire captaincy in 1971 when two journalists, Peter Johnson of the *Daily Mail*, and Howard Booth of the *Daily Mirror*, threw me to the wolves. The Old Trafford Roses match never got out of low gear, Lancashire being dismissed for 168 and Yorkshire replying with 43–2 in thirty-two overs. Johnson and Booth approached me, ostensibly to ask about my dismissal – run out by Clive Lloyd as I attempted to snatch a quick single to get the scoreboard moving. The conversation covered the rest of the day's play and I happened to mention that it had not been easy to score because Peter Lever and Ken Shuttleworth had given the ball a bit too much width. As far as I was concerned I had dealt with the official part of the inquiry and we were talking off the record. To my horror, the headlines next day implied that I had lashed out at the Lancashire bowlers, and the outcry reverberated on both sides of the Pennines for weeks.

Phil Carrick, wary though he was, also learned the hard way how easy it is to fall into a trap, shortly after becoming Yorkshire captain in 1987. The county enjoyed the most successful start to a season in their history, winning two championship fixtures, two Sunday League matches and four Benson and Hedges group ties. This splendid run of results, of course, coincided with my sacking the previous winter, so all the tabloid journalists homed in on Headingley, seeking to put flesh on the bones of a story they had already constructed in their own minds. Carrick cautiously agreed to hold a press conference and gave considerable thought to each answer as he faced a battery of questions. 'Do you think the team is better off without stars?' asked someone. Realizing that this was obviously a disguised reference to my departure from the dressing-room, Carrick tried very hard not to leave a loophole for misunderstanding. 'Obviously having a star player is beneficial so long as he fits into the team,' he replied.

Nothing there to get excited about, he thought, yet at least two headlines screamed 'Good riddance, Boycott' or something very similar the next day, misrepresenting Carrick's low-key observation as an attack on me. Carrick was so angry that he sought legal advice through the club, but it had all been done so cleverly that it turned out not to be worth the trouble of going to court to put the record straight. The hard-nosed representatives of the tabloid press can turn a handful of quotes into almost any story they like, and once an article has appeared a correction is poor compensation. Some of the mud inevitably sticks.

The less responsible newspapers are getting more and more outrageous as they label half-truth and innuendo as 'exclusives', so it is no surprise that the trust which once existed between players and journalists has disappeared. Barrie Meyer, the long-serving Test match umpire and former Gloucestershire wicketkeeper, is a famous victim of the publish-and-be-damned approach. He officiated in the second Test between England and West Indies at Lord's in 1984 and adjudged Viv Richards lbw to Ian Botham on the Saturday. The delivery which removed Richards on 72 did a lot, however, and later on Meyer had some second thoughts. He took the trouble to apologize to Richards that night, admitting that he had considered recalling him. Richards, to his credit, accepted the situation gracefully, although he was probably not too happy about his dismissal. It was a private matter between the two principals and should have remained so, but Meyer happened to mention it over the weekend to a couple of other people involved in the game. A journalist overheard and, unable to resist the temptation, rushed into print with his 'big story', causing trouble where none had existed.

Delving and probing behind the scenes and into the private lives of top sportsmen has become a growth industry, putting more and more pressure on the people at the top. This is grossly unfair as they are subjected to tremendous stress and strain by the competitive nature of their life-styles. These sportsmen are not saints, they are normal human beings in every way except that they have a special talent. They are flesh and blood, and feel hurt just like anyone else when they are crucified on the altar of mass circulation. Occasionally when they tackle a journalist following some particularly vicious attack they get the standard reply: 'You didn't complain when you were praised.' This is a ridiculous defence. Players do not have any voice on what goes in the papers. All sportsmen can do is get on with their job and hope for an accurate report. The press does not do us any favours by recounting how well we have done. It is merely being factual, so when I scored a century I earned due recognition in the public arena for my ability. Journalists covering Yorkshire's matches throughout the 1970s and into the 1980s used to have bets as to who could get Geoff Boycott into the first sentence, even on days when I had not figured prominently in the course of events. They operated on the clear understanding that their editors would be impressed by anything to do with me, and the competition for the biggest headlines and the juiciest stories continues, with truth and integrity the casualties in the circulation war. The press, of course, claims that having your footsteps dogged is the price of fame, yet the newspaper proprietors such as Rupert Murdoch and Robert Maxwell are not avidly discussed in their own or rival publications. I cannot recall reading about their private lives or about their wives and children, even though they are powerful multi-millionaires who affect our lives greatly and exert a tremendous influence over public opinion. Their backgrounds must be at least as interesting as those of the sportsmen their employees hold up for such close examination, but they are presumably protected by the 'dog doesn't eat dog' agreement.

Some newspapers regularly have several reporters covering a Test match, one to keep an eye on the actual cricket and the others literally to 'dig up the dirt' by snooping around the dressing-rooms or the corridors of hotels. Operating as the self-appointed guardians of public morality, they boast about 'investigative journalism', which would be laughable were it not so serious. I realize that people have a natural curiosity about the secrets of the famous, but they do not have any right to be kept informed of what happens off the field. 'Careless talk costs lives,' the Government continually warned throughout the dark days of the Second World War; and now careless reporting can wreck lives.

Even respectable and generous cricket writers find themselves dragged unwillingly into controversy at times, as they were over the Mike Gatting affair. The England captain was pilloried for associating with a barmaid during the first Test against West Indies at Trent Bridge in 1988, when England's achievement in comfortably earning a draw – the first in eleven Tests against the best team in the world – was overshadowed by allegations that two players had taken part in a 'sex orgy'. When Gatting's name was linked with the story, he freely admitted inviting a young woman to his room on his birthday. He strenuously denied that there had been any improper conduct, but he was accused by chairman of selectors Peter May of behaving 'irresponsibly during a Test match' and subsequently sacked as captain.

A lot of players were left to wonder just how much their livelihoods might be affected by the press's interest in events off the field, as nothing in Gatting's behaviour could be said to have undermined England's prospects. On the contrary, the rest of the series fell into a familiar and depressing pattern as England used three other captains, John Emburey, Chris Cowdrey and Graham Gooch, and lost all four matches. Things went from bad to worse when Gooch's appointment for India resulted in that tour being abandoned because of his links with South Africa, and finally when Gatting was denied the captaincy against Australia in 1989. New England supremo Ted Dexter and manager Micky Stewart opted for the Middlesex man, but Ossie Wheatley, chairman of the Test and County Cricket Board cricket committee, vetoed their choice. In doing so he laid himself open to the charge that he had surrendered authority to the media, finding Gatting guilty in a form of trial by television hype and banner headline. It was a crazy decision that left the world at large confused by a ruling body that had done nothing about Gatting's verbal assault on a Test match umpire several months earlier but had condemned him for something that was both private and personal.

The 1987–8 tour to Pakistan had proceeded against a background of open hostility. Chris Broad, the Nottinghamshire opening batsman, received a 'stern warning' from manager Peter Lush for disputing a decision by Shakeel Khan in Lahore, and the weak handling of so serious a breach of discipline established a disagreeable climate, reaching a climax when Gatting confronted Shakoor Rana in a fierce finger-wagging row. The umpire took exception to Gatting supposedly moving a fielder without informing the batsman, a charge the England captain stoutly refuted, going well over the top in his reaction. Within seconds the exchanges got out of hand. The press seized on the incident to drag cricket through the mire, and control slipped from the feeble grasp of the Test and County Cricket Board. The players issued terms for continuing the series and made plain their disgust with the Board.

Gatting eventually paid lip-service to the 'wider interests of the game' by saying he was sorry to the umpire, but the whole business was concluded in a totally unsatisfactory way. Raman Subba Row, chairman of the Board, conceded that Lord's had failed to appreciate the 'extent of the team's problems' and awarded a hardship bonus of £1,000 a head, making a vain attempt to keep this sweetener a secret. It would have been possible to justify the sacking of Gatting over his conduct in Pakistan, but to effectively support him and then get rid of him because of newspaper reports over a barmaid left a sour taste. If the press had been more honourable and dealt only with news of the play, one of the most talented English cricketers would still, I am sure, be representing his country. By turning a socially acceptable form of relaxation into something sordid, the media drove Gatting into the welcoming arms of South Africa and weakened England's resources. As Fred Trueman observed at the time: 'If passing an hour or so with a lady had been an offence in my day, no country would have been able to raise a representative side.'

Either journalists are ignorant of the damage they do, or they don't care. Their activities give substance to the thought in some still open and enquiring minds that professional cricket might not offer all that much in the way of a satisfying career. Teenagers with enough ability to earn selection for Young England are not all that eager to sign on for a job that demands the observance in minutest detail of a unique code of conduct which no young doctor, bank clerk, solicitor or engineer would countenance.

The excesses of the press have been encouraged by the Test and County Cricket Board and the county committees, who, in their efforts to claim more back-page publicity for cricket, have made captains, players and leading personalities far too readily available for interviews. The media have grabbed the opportunity with both hands, increasing their demands as they exploit this development to the full. We have had the gross intrusion of microphones in the ground near the pitch and I await with some trepidation the day when players are asked for their comments between deliveries. These days England captains are obliged to turn up day after day at the close-of-play press conferences, and other players too are regularly called upon to explain their actions during and after the games. What the authorities clearly did not realize when they set the ball rolling was that they could not control the questions, which range from the silly to the dangerous. There is a great difference between a player having a quiet conversation with a trusted journalist and being required to answer difficult questions on the record and often on television when he might still be suffering from the tension and emotions of the match. Tests are showpiece occasions which should advertise all that is best in cricket. The players, and the captain in particular, should be allowed to concentrate on producing their best. Unfortunately, the captain is pressed to defend himself, to justify his decisions and to outline his intentions. 'Why did you change the bowling?' 'Why didn't you change the bowling?' 'Why did you bat first?' 'Why didn't you play a spinner?' Every move is put under the microscope as the captain struggles desperately to please everyone, to be diplomatic and to stay out of trouble.

Gatting's replacement David Gower was far from impressive in the 1989 series with Australia. He made too many mistakes, but his chances of checking his team's slide towards a disastrous defeat were hardly improved by the hostile interrogation he endured from the press every night. The media men even made a big issue of the fact that he slipped away without talking to them one Saturday night, as if it was a criminal offence. It has reached the stage when journalists rely so much on the quote that some simply cannot write a piece without them – even racing correspondents profess to have it straight from the horse's mouth!

The point about cricket, of course, is that captains are cross-examined while the Test is going on, often when the match is delicately poised. Can anyone imagine soccer captain Bryan Robson stopping to give an interview at half-time with England trailing 3–0, or Boris Becker pausing to have a few words when a set down at Wimbledon? I don't think so. Cricket has created a climate in which reporters with no opinions of their own expect the players to do their job for them. To 'dress up' a story, the unscrupulous have been known to drive wedges of suspicion between two captains and their teams by taking quotes out of context from one and repeating them to the other, who has then been persuaded to say something in the heat of the moment which he later regretted.

Ray Illingworth and Richie Benaud were two experienced and cagey captains who handled the press brilliantly. They anticipated trouble and avoided it by manipulating journalists. When it suited their purpose they would make themselves unavailable or slip away quickly, pausing only to say, 'Sorry, nothing to say today, gentlemen.' They also diverted attention from a matter they wanted to keep quiet by releasing an apparently interesting bit of news. 'Did you know about so and so?' they would enquire, well aware that the press would jump in with both feet. Benaud had a newspaper background, however, and Illingworth made an art form of being shrewd. Few captains ever reach their heights, so I would advocate putting the team manager in charge of press relations. He is not under the pressure of playing, and is therefore divorced to a large extent from the emotions and the tension. It is not so easy to criticize him, either, as Brian Clough has pointed out. 'I say what I like as a football manager,' he told me. 'I don't have to score goals on a Saturday. I do the talking and my team does the playing.' That is how it should be at all levels of cricket. Every county has a manager or a coach who could be made responsible for dealing with the press, leaving the captains to get on with the game.

Another area in which the press does cricket – and most other sports, too – a disservice is in knocking down leading personalities. They seem to enjoy creating a personality cult, only to destroy it when it suits their purpose. Don Mosey, one-time *Daily Mail* reporter with Yorkshire before graduating to the BBC, is a classic case. Here is a man who spent countless hours mixing with the Yorkshire players, joining in nightly sing-songs with Don Wilson and Phil Sharpe. He should be doing all he can to help cricket capture the public imagination, but instead he has written two books criticizing individuals who have each put thousands of bottoms on seats all over the country – Geoffrey Boycott and Ian Botham.

For some peculiar reason, certain members of the British press derive pleasure from belittling anyone who has achieved fame and fortune by hard work. It is almost as though they say: 'Right, he's gone far enough. We'll cut him down to size.' Journalists with some knowledge of cricket are entitled to criticize players so long as they are balanced and reasonable. What they are not entitled to do is lash out at individuals and indulge in wild flights of fancy in the furtherance of their careers or to please their sports editors. As a player I would never have dreamed of questioning the captain's decisions. If I had a personal view I kept it to myself or talked it over privately with my team-mates. As a youngster I was taught to follow the captain unquestioningly, so it seems strange to me that the media, although generally ill-informed, should enjoy an opportunity denied to the players. It is no wonder cricketers grow sick of seeing their colleagues made Aunt Sallies for every Tom, Dick and Harry who wants to have a go. A generation has grown up hating the press. Who can blame them?

4

Batting

Sitting back and reflecting on a career that has fulfilled so many of my boyhood ambitions, I cannot help feeling that I would have achieved more had I taken up golf as a profession instead of cricket. Golf is unique among all ball games in that it allows the individual to be the master of his own destiny. When Nick Faldo stands on the first tee in a major championship he knows that the outcome is entirely in his own hands. No-one can snatch the ball away as he swings, or deflect it from the hole when he putts. Success or failure depends entirely on how he alone shapes up to the challenge presented by the occasion and the course.

Compared to cricket, golf is easy. I have said as much to some of the leading golfers I have met when playing in pro–ams and predictably my arguments have been dismissed, but that does not alter my opinion. As an opener for Yorkshire and England I was well aware that one mistake could well mean I would be out. I had to organize my innings, paying careful attention to the tactics of the opposition, to the state of the pitch and to the quality of the bowling. I had to use all my skills in dealing with the good deliveries so that I could score runs from the bad ones. Golfers have to calculate precisely how far they need to hit the ball and take a number of factors into consideration, including the lie of the land, the contours of the green and the pin placings, but they can afford the occasional error. If every golfer had to drop out of a tournament the first time he went one over par, no-one would complete seventy-two holes. No-one has ever won a golf tournament without playing one bad shot and dropping a stroke to par somewhere along the way.

A batsman, on the other hand, gets few second chances if he misjudges the length or line. He cannot recover from a wayward drive by producing an inspired shot from the rough. One momentary lapse, one bit of bad luck and he is out, sometimes run out by a bad call from his partner! I wonder how Faldo would react if someone else snatched the Open from his grasp by playing his ball.

Great sportsmen have certain winning qualities in common: patience, determination, the ability to cut themselves off mentally from others and a phenomenal work rate – to name but a few. I am firmly convinced that I would have won a lot of top tournaments as a golfer, just as I am certain that Ballesteros, Nicklaus or Faldo would have succeeded at cricket had their energies been channelled in that direction from an early age.

The beauty of golf is that you can practise when you want for as long as you want without any restrictions. The legendary Ben Hogan, one of the greatest figures in American golf, raised practice to an art form, being largely self-taught, and I almost imagined it was me when I heard him say: 'I got the greatest satisfaction from practising. It gave me the chance to go out on the tee and forget about everything else but what I was working on that day. There is no greater pleasure than improving.'

As a perfectionist, I recognize the importance of attention to the smallest detail, something that is common sense to the top golfers. Faldo, although consistently achieving a success rate that most other sportsmen would envy, changed his swing in the search for perfection. He subjected himself to eighteen months' hard work and heartache and may well have been tempted to abandon his new swing when things were not going right, but he emerged a much better player.

Golf provides much more opportunity for practice than cricket. All you need is a set of clubs, a bag of balls and a field. It does not matter if the field is pretty rough or what the weather is like. So long as there is daylight, the keen golfer can polish up some aspect of his game. The enthusiastic batsman wanting to do the same has to overcome all manner of obstacles. Even if he has a whole day to spare, he has to find several bowlers and a decent pitch and hope that it does not rain. I wasted so many hours trying to fix up nets; yet had I been a golfer, instead of waiting around for someone to bowl at me, I would have been able to go off alone and practise to my heart's content.

It serves no useful purpose for a golfer to go into a field and hit balls aimlessly, nor does it do anything for a batsman to slog away for fifteen minutes in the nets. Practice should always be undertaken with a purpose. I usually tried to create match conditions by saying to the bowlers: 'I intend to bat for half an hour and you will not get me out. Just as in a game, I will start carefully and gradually build up to take control.' Occasionally, I managed to persuade cost-conscious Yorkshire to provide one or two new balls for the nets because they behave differently from softer, older balls. It hardly helps a specialist opener to practise with a lump of leather that has done service for countless overs when he is likely to face Malcolm Marshall or Curtly Ambrose with something distinctly hard and shiny.

I have spent thousands of hours testing a whole range of theories and ideas in the nets, because that is the place to start the process of becoming a great batsman. I also experimented by attempting different strokes, seeing what happened when, for example, I tried to hit an inswing bowler on the up through the covers. In that way, I utilized every single minute to advantage, although allowances always had to be made for the ability of the bowlers in the nets. I ask young batsmen: 'How do you expect new strokes to pay dividends in a game if you haven't mastered them in the nets?'

It is interesting to note that Ballesteros taught himself to play golf to a very good standard using only one club, which was all he had. Without expensive equipment or the grudging assistance of others, he set about finding out the full extent of his ability. Where the average golfer measures the distances with his eyes and selects what he fondly hopes is the right club, Ballesteros had to manufacture shots, throughout his formative years, learning all the while what the ball would and would not do. This proved to be the best possible practice he could have had.

It did not take county coach Arthur Mitchell long to put me to the test when I arrived at the Yorkshire nets. Although slight and wearing spectacles, I impressed him sufficiently for Fred Trueman to be called up. 'I want you to let it go against this lad and see how he manages,' said Mitchell. Trueman clearly had his doubts, but was quick and hostile enough to give my defence a thorough examination. My pride in getting through that ordeal unscathed also survived the cutting edge of Trueman's tongue. 'Aye, he can defend all right, but he's no strokes,' he said. Mitchell retorted: 'Just think what a batsman he'll be when we teach him to attack.'

Mitchell told me to strengthen my scoring potential on the leg side, so I got some local club bowlers to come to the nets, only to discover that they lacked the essential accuracy, being unable to switch from their normal line around the off stump to attack my pads. By trial and error I came to the conclusion that they would just have to bowl at the stumps while I moved across and took off stump as guard. This meant that I received 70–80 per cent of the deliveries on my pads which enabled me to improve in the correct area.

As an additional bonus I counted any time I was hit on the pad as a dismissal, forcing myself to concentrate hard on not missing the ball and making the most of the situation. You can instil good habits by taking practice seriously, and conversely you cannot expect to be frivolous in the nets and then turn on the concentration like water from a tap. People came to watch me when I practised, but I never spoke to them. I remained in a mental cocoon, seeing and hearing only what I wanted to see and hear.

Self-discipline and a strong, clear mind are vital and those qualities are more important than quantity in terms of practice. It is more productive to work very hard one day and have the next off as a holiday than to turn up on a regular basis and be casual. I have seen Yorkshire and England players mess about for quarter of an hour in the nets, slogging away unconcerned about what happened to the ball. They claimed to have been practising, but really they were wasting their time, going through the motions. When I batted with John Edrich in the West Indies on Colin Cowdrey's tour of 1968, he said of me: 'Geoff makes you play well because he seems so much in charge at his end.' Composure and determination are by-products of sensible preparation. Too many lose interest during practice because they lack concentration. I concentrated for every minute, whether in the nets or out in the middle, whether taking strike or standing at the bowler's end. I tried to work out how long a particular bowler would stay on, how many overs the best bowlers would get through in a session, which fielders might concede runs under pressure and how the pitch was playing. Also, I counted my runs, which helped me to shut out all distractions. I remember batting with Hampshire's Richard Gilliatt in Malaysia on an England 'A' tour and, as we did not have a scorer with us, the local official, a young girl, did duty for both sides. When we came off she proudly informed me that I had scored 154 not out. 'You're wrong there,' I said. 'I got a hundred and seventy-six. You've given Gilliatt twenty-two of my runs. I'm glad you won't be scoring in the first-class games.'

The scoreboard can be used in other ways as an aid to concentration. To avoid becoming complacent, especially if we were doing reasonably well, I used to add a couple of wickets on to the score and reflect on the situation then. There is a great deal of difference between 120–1 and 120–3 and it is surprising how often when one wicket goes down another follows quickly. Gloucestershire's Jack Russell works on a similar principle to keep himself up to the mark. He keeps an eye on his individual total and continually asks himself: 'Would you really like to get out for that?'

Concentration is the key, and without it a batsman is always likely to throw away his wicket. I remember a day–night match in December 1979, between England and Australia at Sydney. We faced Dennis Lillee, Len Pascoe, Rodney Hogg and Geoff Dymock on a decent pitch, but one which had just that little bit in it for the quicks. Australia was restricted to 194–6, a total which indicated accurately the degree of difficulty for the batsmen. The contest was reduced to forty-seven overs a side, so we had a real fight on our hands. Peter Willey helped me to put on 111 for the second wicket. Across the road in the Sydney showground, rehearsals started up for a Rod Stewart concert; this was followed by a speedway meeting and then by a firework display which began with giant rockets whizzing into the night sky. The noise was tremendous, and five wickets went down for 27 runs in no time. In the middle of all this pandemonium Derek Randall marched down the wicket complaining bitterly. 'I can't go on with this banging and crashing. It's impossible to concentrate,' he said. 'Why, what's happening?' I asked. I could, of course, hear the disturbance, but I had shut it out so completely that it represented no more than a hum in the background. 'I'm well established,' I told Randall. 'There's no way I'm going off. We'll win, don't worry – do your best.' He got out for one and gave me a resigned glare as he stalked off with that unmistakable walk of his, but I finished unbeaten on

86 and had Yorkshire wicketkeeper David Bairstow for company as England got home by four wickets with eleven balls to spare.

The secret of concentration is not to let outside factors register. Be aware of them by all means, but keep them outside the mental bubble in which you are operating. Concentration is about channelling your mind into a specific area while directing your energies in one direction. It is not as simple as saying that you will not let your thoughts drift on to what you might be going to do that night or something similar. The mind has to be trained, and there is a lot to be said for building up a regular pattern, starting with homework. This should be done before each day's play and I used to work backwards from the time I wanted to be able to sit down with a nice cup of tea and give myself a short break before the match began. My routine had to account for the possibility that I might be batting straight away, as I would be on the first day 50 per cent of the time. As a matter of habit, I arrived on the ground an hour and a half before the start of play, leaving myself ten minutes to get changed, fifty minutes for exercise and a net and thirty minutes to cool down and think through what the day might have in store.

By always planning ahead I avoided having to rush into a game. It is crazy for a batsman to walk out without giving due thought to the bowlers. Who does what? Which bowlers swing the ball out or in? Is there anyone with a peculiar characteristic? It is possible to be outwitted once – that is human – but anyone falling into the same trap twice is a fool. West Indian Franklyn Stephenson's superb slower ball, which has gained him so many wickets, demands respect. Marshall's bouncer tends to skid through because he is only five foot nine inches, and he has hit a lot of batsmen who did not do their homework. Joel Garner continued to surprise the unwary with his yorker, speared in from something over nine feet. Going back to Mike Procter's lbw hat-trick at Cheltenham, where he bowled round the wicket, it amazed me to see Bill Athey and John Hampshire not offering a stroke, for they should have known that the South African allrounder brought the ball back sharply, forcing batsmen to play at deliveries pitched very much wide of the off stump. Padding up to Procter was asking for trouble.

Being fully prepared was particularly important to me as an opener. I could not enjoy the luxury of sitting in the pavilion watching the early exchanges while I assessed the bowling and the conditions. I had to be ready for anything, as I faced up to the first delivery in nearly every game in which I played. I kept a little black book in which I put notes against the various bowlers who had dismissed me. I thought they would remember how they had got through my defences, and it made sound sense for me to remember as well.

By this simple means I built up a dossier on my leading opponents, and I discovered that some bowlers were easier to score off in certain areas, so a few minutes' homework reading up before a game often paid dividends. I never regarded these notes as being infallible, however, because I had to be flexible and ready to adapt to changing circumstances. Nevertheless, I left as little to chance as possible. It never fails to surprise me when I talk to other cricketers and find that they are not aware of the strengths and weaknesses of other players. They are simply not giving themselves the best chance of doing well. The 1975 men's singles final in the Wimbledon tennis championships stands out as an example of what can be achieved by thoughtful preparation. Arthur Ashe overturned the odds to beat the clear favourite Jimmy Connors because he had devised a plan beforehand. Ashe had lost to Connors often enough to appreciate his power and he knew that the bouncy left-hander liked nothing better than the ball being driven hard at him. Connors used the speed of the ball onto his racket to hammer the ball back, so Ashe countered by gently angling his returns, forcing

Connors to stretch across the court and generate his own pace of return.

I had serious trouble in 1978, after I had broken my left thumb in a one-day international against Pakistan at Old Trafford and missed a string of matches. Pressures put on me by the Yorkshire committee forced me to return before I should have done. Because my left hand was not completely healed, I could not grip properly and my right hand began to take over more and more of the work without my realizing it. When I came back from New Zealand that winter I found that I had slipped into something approaching a two-shouldered stance. This was a real shock to me as I had always had a model stance completely sideways on to the bowler, showing nothing of my right shoulder. I could barely recognize myself on the video. I realized that I needed to take immediate action to get back into the correct position, so I contacted Don Wilson, who is in charge of the indoor school at Lord's. He arranged nets for me morning and afternoon; one of the bowlers was a youthful and distinctly pacy Norman Cowans, at that time making his way towards the Middlesex side. I had to force myself to turn around sideways on and it felt awkward, as though my left shoulder was pointing to extra cover, but in reality I had done nothing more than resume my normal stance. I spent the first few weeks of the season uneasily forcing myself to keep my right shoulder back out of the way, but all the effort brought due reward when I finished the 1979 season with an average of 102.53, to enter *Wisden* as the only batsman to top the three-figure mark twice in an English season.

Nobody's technique, however good, stays with him unless he examines it continually and works at it to keep it finely tuned. As Ballesteros plodded wearily through four months of disappointment in 1989, top coach Bob Torrance pointed out that he was closing the face of the club too much in the back swing. 'I tried hard to cure this weakness, but couldn't,' admitted Ballesteros. Leaving no stone unturned, he read through the instruction books he had himself written and came up with the solution. 'I was standing to the ball too open,' he said, adding, 'Once I closed the stance a fraction I was able to do what Bob wanted me to do. It is very easy to forget the fundamentals. Bob got it half right and I did the rest.'

Cricketers also need to consider changing circumstances, just as the top golfers adapt to the varying demands of links and parkland courses. On their 1980 tour the West Indies brought with them probably the strongest pace attack in history – Andy Roberts, Michael Holding, Joel Garner and Colin Croft – turning the five-match Test series and the three one-day internationals into the equivalent of a commando assault course, which only the bravest survived. It was such a physically demanding situation, with very few deliveries to hit, that all the England batsmen were pushed back on the defensive, with survival the paramount consideration. I had little chance to recover in county cricket, as Yorkshire failed to qualify for the Benson and Hedges knockout rounds and left me out of the Sunday League line-up. I had just one weekend match between each Test, usually on a moderate to poor pitch, which hardly provided adequate opportunity to pick up any batting rhythm.

I felt that my whole approach to batting was being stifled by constant battering from the West Indies bowlers, even though I did reasonably well, winning the Man of the Match award for 70 in the second one-day international at Lord's and averaging 40.88 in the Tests. A universal sigh of relief went up from all the batsmen when the series with West Indies drew to a close, but with the Centenary Test still to come I knew I could not sit back and put my feet up. The Australians had two admirable quick bowlers in Dennis Lillee and Len Pascoe, but two is not four and it did not take a genius to work out that a different approach would be beneficial. England could anticipate the odd bouncer and some top-class bowling from Lillee, but they could also expect with some certainty the chance to make runs and

I wanted to be in shape to claim my share. Once more I telephoned Wilson, who arranged for a pitch to be prepared on the part of the square normally used for the groundstaff side, the Cross Arrows. I batted on that for two days, facing a relay of seamers from the Lord's School operating in pairs from each end which gave me time to think about what I was doing, with other lads fielding out. I put the emphasis on stepping up my feet movement which had been affected by all the bouncer-happy West Indians, and when I asked Wilson what he thought after a couple of sessions he said: 'Well, you look stilted and a bit mechanical – stiff and tense for you.' That represented exactly how I felt, but gradually as I worked at my feet movement the tension eased out of my body to be replaced by a fluidity, and my confidence returned. The difference between the Boycott who arrived at Lord's and the one who left a week later a much happier man was reflected in my scores of 62 and 128 not out in the Centenary Test. I batted really well, losing my wicket only to a magnificent first-innings delivery from Lillee and going on afterwards to make another unbeaten century for Yorkshire at the expense of Derbyshire.

The batsman eager for knowledge can always study the leading players who cross his path. Being a very correct, straight player, I went a long way in cricket without sweeping. When people bowled round about leg stump I would strike the ball towards mid-on or back to the bowler or push defensively if it was not quite there to hit harder. However, I realized after a few years that on certain pitches it would be better if I had a sweep in my armoury. In difficult conditions, when runs were scarce, the opposition would often bring the man up backward of square leg to stop me getting a single for the nudge through the short legs, making it a bit more difficult to keep the score moving. The opposition got used to my not sweeping, so I reasoned that I had better do something to redress the balance. On the 1968 tour to the West Indies I got the chance to study Ken Barrington, Tom Graveney and Colin Cowdrey, three batsmen I admired and respected. Barrington always hit the ball very hard when he swept as with his two-eyed stance he was already partly in position for the stroke, but I could hardly imitate him. I could not get into position quickly enough. Graveney adopted a much more orthodox style, while Cowdrey, altogether a much bulkier figure, stood up and almost paddled the ball down past leg stump. Cowdrey interested me, so I analysed his sweep and came to the conclusion that it was almost impossible for him to get out to the stroke. By compromising between Graveney and Cowdrey, I developed a sweep so that the bat came down and over the ball. There is so much a batsman can do for himself if he has the inclination. It is all a matter of paying attention, of studying the game and asking the right questions of the right people.

Sadly it is just as easy to pick up bad habits, and the technical quality of English batting has declined dramatically in recent years. There is no-one following in the footsteps of classical batsmen such as Len Hutton, Peter May, Colin Cowdrey or my boyhood idol, Tom Graveney. A lot of today's batsmen have had their techniques ruined by using heavy bats. The obsession with heavier bats is inextricably linked with the high backlift, as batsmen strain for extra power. I had all my bats tailor-made at 2lb 5oz., the balance being most important in guaranteeing manoeuvrability. A batsman must be able to control the swing of the bat and it is nonsense to suppose that I could have used the same weight of bat as Botham, who is around a stone and a half heavier, or that a schoolboy could use one of my bats. The bat should feel like an extension of the arm rather than a plank and it should be used as a rapier, not as a cutlass. To play well defensively, a batsman has to be able to adjust at the last fraction of a second which is possible only if the bat is truly a part of him.

Graham Gooch is the leading exponent of the 'new school', standing with his bat above waist height to receive the ball. This method originated with Tony Greig and

David Smith, very tall men well over six feet in height, who discovered that they had to stoop when they were using the normal bat, even with a long handle. For the ideal stance, the batsman is sideways on, nice and comfortable, with his head turned to face the bowler and his eyes level above middle and off stump. If he tilts his head so that one eye slips below the other he cannot focus properly and is slightly overbalanced, so that his judgement is affected around off stump. Greig, in stooping, took his eyes outside the off stump and found it difficult to decide which balls to play and which to leave. After a process of trial and error he decided to hold the bat some six or eight inches off the floor but still in the correct stance so that if his bat had been extended it would have touched the ground. In this way Greig found a solution that worked for him, allowing him to keep his head still and eyes level, at the same time being comfortable. As the bowler ran in, Greig lifted his bat a fraction further to give himself the vital initial momentum for the stroke, whether defensive or attacking. Like a golfer at the start of his swing, the batsman has to have a trigger mechanism, a movement of the hands or bat so that the striking motion is not attempted from a static position.

I have read in a number of coaching books and heard people suggesting on radio and television that it is essential for a batsman to remain as still as possible until the ball has left the bowler's hand. Nonsense. Batsmen must have this trigger mechanism. I moved my right foot back and in the direction of the off stump just before the bowler got into the delivery stride, keeping my weight evenly balanced on the balls of my feet so that I could push off again to play either back or forward. At the instant the ball left the bowler's hand I was absolutely still, just as there is a fraction of a second in a golf swing when the club stops at the top before beginning the descent into the ball. It may be imperceptible, but it is there all the same. Greig started the pick up early, to prevent his body becoming rigid and to guarantee that there would be a rhythm in his batting. Unfortunately,

Gooch came along and exaggerated Greig's sensible touch of improvisation, to stand rather like a baseball player. He is in a hitter's position and, in the absence of more stylish run-makers, Gooch has been copied by county, league and schoolboy cricketers. The baseball striker does not have to defend. He has three chances to hit the ball, and if he fails he is out, so it pays him to be ready to do one thing only – throw the bat at the ball. Batting, however, is not a hitting game, it is an art form, 70 per cent of which is in staying in so that the batsman can score runs from the other 30 per cent of balls that are less accurate. Each batsman is lucky if he averages one and a half runs an over, yet the majority now put the emphasis on attack by holding the bat in the worst possible way for a defensive stroke.

When I played defensively the bat never got above stump height at any stage. A short backlift and a short downswing gave a control that is denied to Gooch and those like him as they slow down to minimize the impact of bat on ball. It is incomprehensible to me that qualified coaches should teach children to stand to receive the ball with the bat waving about in the air; and it is wrong when they teach kids to play from a static position, pushing out the front leg and the bat at the same time. The bat should be picked up as the bowler bowls, and the foot should arrive to the pitch of the ball fractionally before the bat.

No other high-quality Test batsman anywhere in the world uses the Gooch method. The only players who can gain any benefit from his approach are tail-enders in limited-overs games, whose sole aim is to slog the ball as far as possible.

Cricket offers no prizes to the man who can hit the ball hardest or furthest. Batting is not a matter of getting in one big, successful effort like an Olympic javelin or hammer thrower; it is about repeating attacking and defensive strokes correctly. If I entered a big-hitting competition with Ian Botham there would be only one winner. Botham is a powerfully built man, but I submit that quite a few of us, especially the peerless Don Bradman, have proved that control and timing rather than brute strength hold the key to consistent run-making. Bradman, a genius and twice as good as any other batsman, was slightly built and used a very light bat to accumulate 6,996 Test runs for an average of 99.94. Len Hutton's runs flowed gracefully from little more than a schoolboy-sized bat. Yes, there are magic moments encapsulated in tremendous feats of hitting strength, Botham's ruthless destruction of the Australians at Headingley in 1981 being a spectacular example, but the aim of the batsman in first-class cricket should be to stay in and not make mistakes while picking up the runs at every reasonable opportunity. The former Somerset captain Peter Roebuck once wittily observed that, when batting at number four for the county, his principal objective was to stay in long enough to prevent Viv Richards and Botham, at three and five in the order, becoming involved in a partnership. If they did get together Botham in particular would try to despatch the ball higher and harder than Richards, a pointless exercise which often brought his downfall.

Golfers need to hit the ball a long way to compete in major championships. They sometimes have to try to reach the par fives in two, but they do not stand with the club around their ears, nor do they clench their teeth and lash out with all their might. Boris Becker does not prepare to receive service brandishing his racket above his head either.

Anyone who excels at any ball game appreciates the virtues of rhythm and timing, the former for control and the latter for power. Ballesteros strikes the ball over such huge distances with apparent ease because his timing is immaculate. A batsman can never score more than six runs anyway, however fierce the shot, and however fast the ball might be travelling when it reaches the boundary.

As a batsman gets older, his reflexes and eyes deteriorate and it is easy to lose the desire to play cricket. Concentration becomes more difficult, and I was interested to hear Viv Richards say that he had lost his edge after England's tremendous victory in the 1990 Jamaica Test. He has been regarded as the best batsman in the world for twelve years or more and few people question his standing in the game, so it was a big admission for him to make. He was thirty-eight at the time, and I thought he had been short of his very best form for a couple of years. Richards, proud of his reputation, enjoyed producing spectacular strokes, relying on his marvellous co-ordination and on his ability to see the ball very early. Gradually, however, like the rest of us, he began to experience difficulty in dominating the bowling. Age crept up on him gradually, so that for a while he did not really notice that things were not quite as easy. All great players have been through the same experience, being hit one day by the sickening realization that they were past their best.

In the West Indies Graham Gooch spoke to me about the same thing, partly, I suspect, because he remembered those two series in 1980 and 1981 when we both batted superbly against the finest quartet of fast bowlers in the history of the game – Michael Holding, Colin Croft, Joel Garner and Andy Roberts. His 123 at Lord's in 1980 must come close to being the best innings of his life, and for forty minutes he had the West Indies' attack in the palm of his hand. He got himself into a position of complete control before they regrouped and forced him back on to the defensive. Very few people can have been so much in command against such formidable bowling, but as we talked in 1990 Gooch confessed that he could no longer do the things that had come so naturally then. At the height of his powers he had grown accustomed to dominating county attacks, being encouraged to try to do the same in Tests, but once he passed the pinnacle of his physical powers he had to acknowledge unwelcome limitations.

Flaws in his technique added to his problems, while mine held me in good stead. In my last season with Yorkshire I had a championship average of 52.35 as a forty-five year old, and felt confident of playing on for another two years or so had I not been sacked. I hated the physical deterioration taking place, but I worked hard to cope with it, keeping my mind cool and analytical. In that way I shaped my batting to meet the circumstances as they were rather than how I wished they might have been. I cut out several shots and kept things as simple as possible. The hook, for example, virtually disappeared, although from time to time I tried to get it back in the nets.

It is natural to challenge the advancing years, which is why Richards gets out to extravagant shots. Once he could get away with these; now, all too often, he can't. I doubt if he will ever accept restraints on his talent. His macho image means too much to him, and even when the odds are stacked against him he will have a go rather than adjust his thinking.

Richards actually became the victim of some spectacular, even silly, failures. When he was at his peak and in the course of long and generally disciplined innings he put together some strokes that were unbelievable and outrageous, but in the later years he has found it difficult to concentrate sufficiently. Thus he attempts too much too soon. It seemed to me that the penny had not dropped as England and West Indies battled it out in 1990, although his performance was also affected by illness. Privately he admitted that he could not shut out the distractions. He sweats a lot, which is healthy in one way, but it can increase the irritation level out in the middle, especially on very hot days, so he actually needs very strict mental discipline. It would be a pity if such a fine batsman were to be remembered largely for a series of brisk cameo innings because he failed to come to terms with the realities of growing older.

Richards by the slightest of margins is the second best batsman I played against, Gary Sobers being slightly better. He will always be capable of making runs, but he cannot hope to dominate as he did before when he continues to give the bowlers too many chances. He needs to approach things in a different way, as Gooch realized after being exposed by the Australians. He went to the West Indies working hard to improve his technique, becoming more orthodox and less flamboyant. It is all about application and common sense.

Facing fast bowling can be summed up in one word – fear. The fear of getting hurt, the fear of being put in hospital; that is what is at the back of every batsman's mind whether he is playing in Tests, the championship or in the leagues. Without courage, therefore, he is lost, no matter how good his technique might be. The best-looking player in the world is not going to make runs against real pace if deep down he is afraid. He will be beaten before he takes his guard. One thing is for certain, the pacemen will soon find out if he lacks the courage to take them on. The crux of facing fast bowling is knowing that you are going to get hit. You cannot avoid being hit; it is part of a professional batsman's job.

All ball sports create injuries – it is inevitable. Footballers get stud marks down their legs, rugby players take hard knocks as part of their normal routine. Batsmen are no different. They have to get used to the fact that a cricket ball is hard and it can hurt. All the best players have taken a blow on the body at some time or another. It is no 'big deal'. The batsman who wants to succeed must be prepared to accept pain. Maurice Leyland, the great Yorkshire left-hander from the pre-War era, gave me some sound advice in my early days at the county nets. 'Nobody likes fast bowling, but some of us didn't let on,' he said. Fred Trueman, who knew as much about fast bowling as any man who ever lived, also helped me to adopt the right mental attitude. Not long after I earned my place in the Yorkshire team he told me: 'You'll play for England one day, young man.' This both pleased and surprised me. 'I hope so, but I've only just got into county cricket,' I replied. 'Don't worry, you'll play for England all right,' insisted Trueman, 'and I'll tell you something. You'll get hit. You cannot avoid it. When you do, pick yourself up, dust yourself down and carry on.

Keep your mouth shut because if you give the fast bowlers any lip there'll be only one winner and it won't be you.' That was the best advice I ever got about playing fast bowling and it helped to give me composure.

Many batsmen allow themselves to be ruffled when they are hit, which is silly. Alec Stewart, of Surrey, batted beautifully in a lengthy net session during the preparations for the West Indies tour until he misjudged a ball from Gladstone Small, who worked up a good pace by bowling from twenty yards rather than twenty-two. Stewart took a sharp blow on the chest, and from that moment lost all confidence. He poked and prodded, played and missed, and edged to slip.

The first thing a batsman must do after being hit is take his time and ignore everyone else. The fielders may be sympathetic, but the bowler certainly will not. He will be looking instead to see how the batsman reacts. If the batsman allows himself to be hurried back to the crease he is likely to make a bad shot. The ball that actually hits a player does not often get him out, but it may well soften him up and cause his downfall soon afterwards. Many times I have heard it said in the dressing-room: 'It was the ball before that got him out,' as a batsman trudges disconsolately back from the middle. There is nothing that the fielding side or the umpire can do to make the batsman resume before he is ready. I did not get hit very often, but when I did I made sure that I regained my composure before starting again. Occasionally the umpire indicated that I should get on with the game, but I always said: 'No, wait a minute. That hurt and I'm not ready.' Even if the bowler has started his run-up to the stumps, the batsman should not hesitate to draw away if he feels unhappy. If that makes the bowler angry, too bad. Golfers walk away from the ball when they are distracted and so should batsmen.

Once play does re-start, there is no need for the batsman to slam the ball to the boundary or to adopt an aggressive attitude. A few minutes of solid defence will establish clearly that he is back in control of the situation. Simply by displaying sound judgement in the selection of stroke will make a statement to the bowler. The worst thing a batsman can do is to lose his temper or let his heart rule his head. There is no doubt that a person must have passion to become a great sportsman. He must care deeply about what he is doing, but that passion should be channelled into productive areas. Obviously your heart races and the adrenalin flows when the pressure is on, but the successful batsman remains cool and calculating. If he lets his emotions get the better of him and stops thinking, then he is lost.

The press nicknamed Bjorn Borg the 'Ice Man' at the height of his power, when he loomed like a giant over Wimbledon. His calm authority stemmed from an important lesson early in life. Already established as a prodigy, he threw a tantrum on court, so his mother took away his racket for a month. That hard decision did Borg an immense favour. He never lost his temper again and rarely displayed a hint of temperament. There was time to relax when he had won, and then he shrugged off the shackles of restraint, going down on his knees or holding aloft his arms in salute to the ranks of his adoring fans. Steve Davis has made himself the most successful snooker player of all time by keeping a tight grip on himself, potting with clinical efficiency and calculating the angles for his safety play with machine-like accuracy. Someone wrote that he was more like a cleverly designed robot than a human being; I consider that a tribute to his professionalism.

The clearest way to inform the bowler and the fielder crouched almost within touching distance that whatever they do you are equal to it is to continue with your normal game. Let them see that you are not worried. Some batsmen, bristling with aggression, say in the dressing-room: 'If he stands there when I get in I'll shift him.' That, to me, is allowing the bowler to impose himself on you. I reasoned that if I hit the ball hard at the fielder in an attempt to frighten him I might lose four runs or the ball might fly in the air to be caught by another player. Either way I would lose out. It paid me to play naturally, for when the right ball came I could put it away to the boundary firmly enough to remind the fielder I could cause him some pain if I wanted to. That thought alone was enough to make all but the bravest and most agile fielders rock back on their heels a bit.

There was a notable championship match at Middlesbrough in 1974 when Middlesex bowled Yorkshire out on a pitch that turned a bit without being anything like unplayable, although we failed twice and lost by an innings. Mike Brearley had not been captain of Middlesex all that long and he stationed himself close in on the off side to Fred Titmus, who was getting a bit of bite with his off-spinners. 'I don't want you there,' said Titmus, who knew me much better than did Brearley. 'It's all right, I'm fine,' insisted Brearley, much to the amusement of slip Peter Parfitt and wicketkeeper John Murray. 'No, you're better off away from there,' insisted Titmus, who, having been on two tours with me to South Africa and Australia, knew well enough that his captain was right in my hitting area. Perhaps because he had not been captain very long, Brearley stood his ground, even though Titmus added: 'You're putting *me* off more than him.' Sure enough, after a handful of deliveries I drove Titmus for four very close to Brearley, who bristled: 'You tried to hit me then.' 'Listen,' I told him, 'if I'd wanted to hit you I would have done. Don't have any doubts about that.' 'I told you not to stand there,' said Titmus, well aware that Brearley had put himself effectively out of the game and that he would not get me caught in that position.

The same principles apply against the pacemen and even in the heat of a Test match I refused to be intimidated or to accept the domination of any bowler. I played the ball where I thought it should be played. Michael Holding was the fastest bowler I faced. We referred to him respectfully as 'whispering death' as he glided in on his approach, his feet hardly seeming to touch the ground. At Lord's in 1980 he produced exceptional pace even by his high standards. England got bowled out cheaply and the West Indies batted to build a big lead before leaving us with a torrid hour on the Monday night. Holding, having had a long rest, really steamed in, reinforcing his stifling clutch of fielders around the wicket by calling up Clive Lloyd from cover to menace me from short point. Fortunately, the pitch was good and runs did not enter the calculations. All that mattered was getting through to the close and the next day. It was one of the best hours I ever played: everything hit the centre of the bat. Receiving a few throat balls I dropped them down at my feet, and made Clive bend down to pick up the ball. I did not have to be clever, to kick the ball away or make some smart comment. The message got across loud and clear.

To deal effectively with fast bowling, especially in the West Indies, a batsman has to be literally on his toes, or at least on the balls of his feet, just like a boxer. I got ready to combat speed by working out in the dressing-room just before I went in to bat. It is essential to be ready for the first ball – you can't expect a gentle sighter! I jumped up and down, waving my arms and twisting my trunk to make sure I was warmed up. It amused me to see Martyn Moxon, with whom I opened the Yorkshire innings towards the end of my career, standing in front of the mirror combing his hair and straightening his collar before we went out. 'I want to look nice and neat,' he said, but as I pointed out he could hardly hope to remain tidy if I pushed the first ball for a hard-run three. I was interested more in how I felt than how I looked and I wanted to be loose in case the first ball happened to be aimed at my head like a guided missile travelling at ninety miles an hour or more. Nobody is going to look 'nice and neat' if Ambrose or Marshall 'parts your hair'. Under pressure from top-class pacemen a batsman has to keep moving, and the first time he can enjoy the luxury of relaxing is when he is back in the pavilion. As the boxing referees say: 'Be ready to defend yourself at all times.' No matter how many runs you may have made, the next ball is a potential killer, and like Fred Astaire I never stopped dancing.

It is fatal to become flat-footed. Fast footwork is, in fact, much better protection against fast bowling than the helmet. The fad for wearing reinforced headgear has definitely made batsmen lazy, and it is incredible to see county cricketers ducking and turning the back of their heads to the bowler. No wonder they get hit. Long before helmets were invented, good batsmen kept their eyes on the ball until the last split-second and then took evasive action, still watching and still in control until it passed over their shoulder to the wicketkeeper or in front of their face.

I finally decided to wear a helmet against the really quick bowlers because to continue without one might have suggested that I was throwing down the gauntlet. In my fortieth year I saw no merit in antagonizing the most lethal fast-bowling attack in the world, the West Indians. I did not want to give them an extra excuse for peppering me with the short stuff. Most of them did not need one as it was. They wanted badly to get me out and be rid of me. There is no doubt in my mind that in normal circumstances batsmen would be much better advised to forget about helmets and rely on watching the ball more closely, while staying sideways on to the bowler to present a limited target. The sight of helmets being brought out for some medium-paced trundler is pathetic. It cannot be coincidence that more batsmen are getting hit than ever before. This is not just the case in Test cricket, either. Average seam bowlers are doing a lot of damage. Helmets do offer an essential degree of additional protection against the genuinely fast bowlers, but they also give batsmen a false sense of security, so that they no longer concentrate on basic technique by keeping their eyes on the ball as it passes them and goes over their shoulders. Too many players just duck when they see the ball knocked in short and leave themselves hostages to fortune. They are not watching, so if the ball does not bounce as much as they expect, or if it seams back at them, they get hit. I appreciate that inconsistent bounce does play a part in the number of injuries sustained in recent years, but that is only part of the story. I focused on the ball until the last possible split-second and rarely got hit on the body.

In fact, I suffered only two serious injuries in my career. The first was disc trouble, sustained against Australia at Edgbaston in 1968, but Paddy Armour, who has a clinic in Wakefield, put me right and helped me stay fit afterwards. Then Graham McKenzie broke my left arm in Australia in 1971, when I was in tremendous form and he delayed my début as the Yorkshire captain. Despite facing so much fast bowling over twenty-five years, I have rarely been hit on the head. Rodney Hogg caught me a glancing blow in 1978, the ball going for four leg byes. Rather more seriously, Dennis Lillee clipped me on the chin early in my innings when I went on afterwards to make 137 at the Oval in 1981. I swayed back to allow a delivery to pass across the front of my face, but it seamed back and followed me which was not very pleasant, although I watched the ball until the last split-second. A very similar incident occurred at Sheffield in 1982, when Kent's Graham Dilley struck me on the chin; I also went on to make a century then. West Indian paceman Colin Croft went around the wicket and aimed at my body more than once, getting through my defences at the Oval in 1980 to hit me and cut my left eye.

But my biggest frustrations have been damaged fingers. Finger injuries are annoying because you expect the padding on the batting glove to protect you, but in fact these are an occupational hazard, particularly so far as openers are concerned, for they face the new ball when the bowlers are fresh and hostile. Around 1979 I started to wear plastic on the top of the fingers of the gloves, taping on Plastizote from hospitals and I never had any further problems. Had I known about this earlier I could have avoided a few broken fingers, and more glove manufacturers should use this technique. So often when I had a damaged finger that did not heal as quickly as expected I was pilloried for not being available, the suggestion being that I did not want to play. I cannot imagine a bigger piece of nonsense, for I have always been keen to play whenever I was in a position to do myself justice. I saw no virtue in playing when not fit, although the Yorkshire committee and the England selectors did not always agree.

The best players are often pressed to play when they are not really fit enough and resentment can build up on both sides, which is sad. I missed Yorkshire's 1972 Benson and Hedges Cup Final defeat by Leicestershire after my finger had been damaged by a ball from Bob Willis and, although there was no chance of my turning out at Lord's except as a one-handed passenger, I noticed a few funny looks.

There are times when things go badly wrong for any sportsman, no matter how talented or successful he might be, and it is then that he needs strength of character. Some people call it bloody-mindedness, but really it is the refusal to give in, the determination to stay afloat when you think you are drowning. When a batsman reaches the stage when he cannot imagine where his next run is going to come from, it is much easier to give up, to get back to the dressing-room, where he will be safe from the critical gaze of the public. The difficult part is walking out to the wicket to face the possibility of another failure. Spectators do not understand that part of the game. They remember the good times and imagine that life is always easy. Well, when you are out of form and you have to face the likes of Holding, Roberts, Garner and Croft you need all the character in the world. Your resolve is tested to the full. At those moments the burning question is: 'How badly do you want to succeed?' It is as simple as that. If you really want to be a great batsman, if you are driven by the burning desire to be the best, then you fight your way through the difficulties. Even when you are holding on by your finger-tips you start climbing the mountain again, somehow finding the spirit to keep going.

I suppose one of the low-water-marks in my career was in 1981, when I made nought and one in the Test against the West Indies at Kensington Oval, Bridgetown. In the first innings Holding bowled one of the fastest overs in the history of cricket; his last ball plucked out my off stump and sent it cartwheeling twenty yards. A strange silence settled briefly on the ground before pandemonium broke loose with thousands of people jumping up and down. In the second innings I was only a whisker away from getting a pair.

With the next Test only nine days away, I had precious little time in which to regain my form and confidence, and I could not turn my back on the situation. The only way forward was to apply my mind to redressing the balance. I sought out Michael Blakey, a Yorkshire-born journalist covering the tour for the BBC, and he agreed to set up a television in his hotel room so that I could study the video of Holding's fateful over. I sat through those six balls time and time again, slowing and stopping the film until I had learned everything there was to know about the over. The next step was to practise and the three-day match against the Leeward Islands provided what I hoped would be an ideal opportunity. I did get 72 in the first innings but then was run out, which did not help. Then, at the second attempt, I got 15 before falling victim to the worst lbw decision of my life. The first delivery from off-spinner Guishard, bowling wide of the crease, pitched a long way outside the line of the stumps, and almost as a reflex action I kicked it away. The bowler appealed and the umpire raised his finger. I could not believe my eyes, but I had to go all the same. I felt angry and sick at being denied the chance to work on my batting and wondered just what else could go wrong as I reached the pavilion. As I sat in the big open window having a drink of water, one of the attendants began jumping up and down, shouting for another wicket, pointing at me and laughing. I threw some of the water at him in sheer annoyance and when he continued to taunt me I threw some more. He, in turn, picked up a brick, aimed at the window, and was prevented from attacking me only by the intervention of some others. Incredibly, the man, who was called Lea, said he wanted to press assault charges against me, calling as a witness a Detective-Sergeant Lewis, who, on duty to protect the England team, had seen the incident.

The police officer had to confirm that I had thrown water, although he informed us that Lea was a well-known local trouble-maker. The local police commissioner and our tour manager, Alan Smith, became involved, asking me to apologize. 'No way,' I said firmly. 'He had no right to behave like that in our special enclosure, deliberately provoking me.' Smith's concern centred on the fact that I could have gone to prison, possibly for a week or two, if I had been found guilty, but I was in no mood to back down, although I did not like the idea of 'doing time'. Lea appeared keen to pursue the matter and eventually I agreed that I had been wrong to throw the water. The police commissioner put some pressure on Lea, saying: 'Come on, let's all be big men. Speak up, man, and accept Mr Boycott's generous apology.' Grudgingly he did so, muttering something about being sorry himself, and I flew off to Antigua for the fourth Test with the rest of the party. The whole business amused my team-mates, Derbyshire's Geoff Miller pointing out: 'You might have been rolling the wicket for us on our next visit,' which was a reference to the fact that they use convicts from the local prison for this task. Ian Botham, captain on that trip, invited me to join his club. 'I have a court case coming up at home,' he said. I spent a lot of time in the nets in the two days before the Test, making up for 'lost time', and the rest is history. I took an unbeaten 104 off the West Indies to save the game on a good pitch, playing one of the best mind-over-matter innings of my career. As he passed me in the course of a long and frustrating day for his side, Holding paused to say: 'A different day, a different game, Geoffrey.' His comment said it all and showed what a nice guy he is.

5

Better Tests

Test cricket is being ruined by an excess of fast bowling, and unless something is done to bring back variety the game will suffer. As an opening batsman for twenty-five years facing up to some of the most hostile attacks in history, I appreciate that there must be a physical element in the contest between bat and ball. Courage has to play a part if cricket is not to become a game for namby-pambies and I accept without reservation that there is a place for the short ball, no matter how fast the bowler. Unless the bowler can use the bouncer as a legitimate tactic, front-foot players will have an easy time and batsmen lacking courage will make a lot more runs than they should, which cannot be right. I went into first-class cricket in the 1960s, when there were no helmets, and padding often amounted to no more than a rolled-up towel strategically fastened around the chest or the thigh. In those days if a batsman couldn't handle fast bowling he hit out before he got out, and this applied particularly to tail-enders. All the pacemen dropped one or two short enough to keep the batsmen wary and prevent them lunging permanently on to the front foot. The bouncer was a surprise weapon; no-one made better use of it than Fred Trueman, who usually followed up with a very fast yorker. Trueman, of course, teamed up for England with Brian Statham to form a Roses combination which tested the nerve of batsmen around the world; as did Nottinghamshire's Harold Larwood and Bill Voce before the War. Other famous partnerships included Wes Hall and Charlie Griffith of the West Indies; Dennis Lillee and Jeff Thomson of Australia; Peter Heine and Neil Adcock of South Africa; and, of course, Ray Lindwall and Keith Miller, the strike force for Don Bradman's superb 1948 Australians. On the other hand great fast bowlers such as John Snow, Bob Willis, Frank Tyson, Peter Pollock, Mike Procter, Richard Hadlee and Imran Khan were forced to carry the fast-bowling attack on their own for most of their careers.

All were very tough competitors and Peter Richardson, the Worcestershire opener, suffered a typical experience at the hands of Heine during the 1956–7 series in South Africa. Richardson marked his first appearance against South Africa by scoring 117 at Johannesburg. His satisfaction at that achievement was, however, marred because during his innings Heine had hit him on the head. Without a helmet, he slumped to the ground almost unconscious. As he lay on the floor, dazed, trying to refocus and surrounded by worried fielders, all Richardson could hear was Heine's voice saying: 'Get up, get batting and I'll hit you again.' The bowler had no sympathy for the batsman and Heine had a reputation for being a very hard man indeed.

Fast bowlers today are no better, no quicker, no more dangerous than they were in the past, but there are more of them. Where once the normal composition of a Test attack was one or two pacemen, two spinners and an allrounder, who often bowled at medium-pace, now we have four West Indian fast bowlers, who share the day's reduced allocation of overs and hammer away relentlessly. The arrival on the scene of Australian Kerry Packer's World Series cricket in the 1970s brought about the big change. He signed up many of the best players in the world, many of whom were bowlers of well above average pace. There was no point in paying them to act as spectators, so they all played and even Derek Underwood, one of the greatest slow bowlers of any generation, hardly got more than a handful of overs. At the same time, the leading fast bowlers began to realize that bouncers above head height or wide of the body were a waste of time and effort when bowling to top-class batsmen. It takes a lot more out of a bowler when he bangs the ball in short, so the pacemen began to aim at specific targets – the ribs, the heart, the shoulders and the neck – areas in which it is difficult for the batsman to play correctly.

The mechanics of the situation are simple. If the ball lifts no more than chest height, the Test batsman should be able to get his hands in the proper position to play it down safely, but if it bounces that bit more it is impossible to get on top of the stroke. When the ball is travelling around ninety miles an hour the decision whether to play or take evasive action has to be made in a fraction of a second. There is always the risk of serious injury if the batsman gets it wrong because the ball is aimed at those vulnerable parts of the body – the head, ribs and heart. It is a form of attacking bowling, and it does not offer the batsman much scope. The only positive response would be to hook, but this shot is fraught with danger, and if the hook is ruled out the cricket becomes very dull from the spectators' point of view. From the late 1970s, therefore, a modern form of bodyline developed naturally, with all the Packer teams having three or four fast bowlers wearing down the batsmen. It was not planned like Douglas Jardine's assault on the Australians in the 1932–3 series in Australia, but it had much the same effect. Jardine managed to reduce Bradman's average from 100 to 56.5 which was regarded as a major triumph, and England won the series 4–1. Jardine had only Larwood and Voce. The West Indies, on the other hand, have regularly employed four fast bowlers. Although the West Indies has enjoyed the most success, the emphasis on pace is now universal. Allan Border, the Australian captain, went on record during the 1988–9 series against Viv Richards' team to say that while he and his players did not like being on the receiving end of the short stuff they would do just the same if they had the fire-power.

Border was speaking from the heart after being put under a lot of pressure by Curtly Ambrose. Most left-handers do well against the pacemen because the ball's natural line is across rather than at them and they are not in so much physical danger. The position is much the same as it is for right-handers against left-arm over the wicket. As an outstanding batsman, Border represented a serious challenge to the West Indians, so Ambrose went after him, hammering in the ball at his ribs with two men up in close-catching positions, one at forty-five degrees and one at short-square. He also stationed one man at fine leg for the hook and another at mid-wicket, saving the single. The difficulty for Border was that he had nowhere to hit the ball, as Ambrose did not pitch anything up or put anything wide enough on the off to give room for the left-hander's slash, square-cut or off-drive. Dean Jones approached me and said that Border would like a chat if I could spare the time. I knew straight away what he wanted to discuss and what he would have to do to combat a form of attack he had not experienced before. He had never worn an arm pad, face mask or chest protector before, so I advised him to change his policy. I told him to turn round very slightly towards the bowler and then let Ambrose hit him a few times on his chest pad. By doing this and refusing to hook, while concentrating on staying in, he forced Ambrose to abandon what was becoming a pointless exercise and to change his direction, thus giving Border the opportunity to pick up some runs on the off side.

That, though, was a short-term solution to an ongoing problem that has been the subject of much debate, and various attempts have been made to curb the power of the fast bowlers. One of the silliest involved a code of conduct drawn up by the captains and umpires, which prevented bowlers dropping short against players designated as non-batsmen. This crazy idea followed an unfortunate incident at Edgbaston during the 1978 series against Pakistan when Willis hit Iqbal Qasim in the mouth, causing a wound which required two stitches.

Willis was strongly criticized for going around the wicket and letting go a bouncer to a tail-ender acting as 'night-watchman', but the Pakistani left-hander had resisted for almost an hour, frustrating the England attack and protecting his more accomplished colleagues while the bowlers were fresh. The incident therefore raised several arguments. Down the years most fast bowlers abided by the unwritten law that restricted short-pitched deliveries to the specialist batsmen well able to take care of themselves, but that was a period when those down the order slogged cheerfully at anything they could reach. Possibly because there is so much one-day cricket, bowlers have begun to pay more attention to their batting and many, like Qasim, are sufficiently competent to hang about.

I could not see any sense in the horse-trading that went on when Mike Brearley's 1978–9 tourists arrived in Australia. It was decided that bowlers could bounce only recognized batsmen, and lists were duly drawn up separating those who could expect a free ride and those who would have to face the music. Inevitably things got out of hand. Rodney Hogg, who had a reputation as a tearaway fast bowler, chipped in with 36 and 16 in the first Test at Brisbane, top-scoring in the first innings after his side had been 53–7. He wore neither helmet nor chest pad, confident that as he had been designated a non-batsman he was in no danger. This did not please Ian Botham, who in the Australian second innings, after a tussle with Hogg when batting himself, said: 'He's going to get some around his ear.' 'You can't do that, I've agreed with Graham Yallop that Hogg isn't a batsman,' said Brearley. 'I don't care,' insisted Botham. 'He's going to get some of his own medicine.' 'I'm telling you that you've got to pitch it up,' said Brearley. 'Why, who's going to stop me dropping short?' asked Botham, receiving plenty of vocal support from me and the rest of the England batsmen.

Obviously, by the time any lower-order player has collected twenty or thirty runs he has to accept the full treatment because he may start to have an influence on the outcome of the game and today, with full protection from a helmet and specially designed chest and arm padding, a tail-ender is very unlikely to get hurt. There are, I admit, exceptions and Geoff Lawson had his jaw broken against West Indies in the second Test at Perth in 1988, but he went in without a face mask, so his injury was his own fault, particularly as the delivery from Curtly Ambrose was not so short. When top-class batsmen wear masks it does not make sense for a bowler to bat without one. That incident provoked howls of protest from some sections of the media and from the public, but the most sensible comment came from John Dyson, Lawson's New South Wales team-mate and a former Australian opener, who was watching on television. Before Lawson had been hit, Dyson asked: 'What the heck is Henry [Lawson's nickname] doing facing those guys without a mask?' Dyson instinctively recognized the dangers; properly protected, Lawson would have been quite safe.

Drawing up arbitrary lists of those who can and cannot be subjected to bouncers without any regard to the circumstances of a particular match does nothing to improve the quality of Test match cricket, nor would drawing a line across the pitch and insisting that the ball be pitched beyond it. How can the same line be reasonable for batsmen who might well be very different in height? How can the line be moved when the ball becomes older and softer or when the pitch becomes easier or more difficult? Another non-starter is the scheme to lengthen the pitch to twenty-four yards. Such a move would definitely make life more difficult for the pacemen, but it would also destroy the spinners, turning them into useless lob bowlers. Restricting bowlers to one bouncer per over does not work either. Under that arrangement the batsman would know he was safe once the ball had been dropped short, and all sorts of arguments would follow if a delivery fractionally short brought a wicket as the batsman played confidently forward under the impression that everything would be right up to him. A tremendous row would develop if a batsman lobbed a catch off the splice, only to be given not out on a matter of a few inches in the ball's trajectory.

The trouble is that all these ideas have not been thought through logically. The only sensible solution is bound up with over-rates. The West Indies average barely twelve overs an hour which is ridiculous. By slowing down the game they give their quartet of fast bowlers plenty of rest between overs, and by getting through little more than twenty-four overs in a session they ensure that each bowler has to contribute a maximum of six – a total of eighteen in a day. The bowlers stay relatively fresh and the batsman is prevented from getting into any sort of rhythm. There is a long, tedious delay between deliveries; sometimes when Michael Holding and Colin Croft were bowling at each end, sauntering leisurely back to their marks, I felt I had time to watch a John Wayne western in between balls. England have been pushing for a minimum of sixteen overs an hour for a long time, only to be defeated by the block votes of the other members of the International Cricket Conference. This, though, is a very reasonable target and I would make it the minimum requirement.

I do not believe in imposing financial penalties for slow play. The West Indies would either pay them out of their winnings or, I suspect, might ignore them at the end of a tour, heading home with the debts left behind them. As with the championship, I would add 10 runs in the form of extras to the total for every over below a minimum thirty-two in each session. Thus, the West Indies with their twelve overs an hour would hand over 80 runs at the break for lunch

Mark Ramprakash
batting for Middlesex
against Worcestershire
in the 1988 NatWest
Trophy final. He needs
to adopt a more
disciplined approach if
he wants to make big
scores consistently.

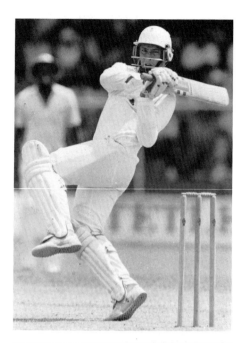

Nasser Hussain, seen here hooking in the one-day international at Bridgetown, Barbados **(top)**, impressed briefly on England's 1990 tour of the West Indies, but he must learn to curb his tendency to open the face of the bat, as he does here **(bottom)** in the fifth Test in Antigua, if he is to develop into a genuine Test batsman.

Alec Stewart showed
a lot of courage
against the West
Indies pacemen on the
1990 tour, but over
and over again he
chased the ball wide
of the off stump,
playing well away
from his body. Unless
he cuts out these
shots, his future
in Test cricket is
limited.

Robert Bailey, seen here both giving and receiving, disappointed on the 1990 West Indies tour. Unless he improves his technique it is doubtful whether he will make it at the highest level.

Richard Blakey is one young batsman who sought my advice last winter and prospered with some big scores on the England 'A' team tour of Zimbabwe.

Michael Atherton, another young player who did well in Zimbabwe. An intelligent batsman, he has improved his feet movement and with this his balance.

Tim Curtis scores runs regularly for Worcestershire, but his technique is inadequate against Test-class bowling. Here he falls lbw to Terry Alderman in the fifth Test against Australia at Trent Bridge in 1989.

There is no substitute for getting the technical basics right. Kim Barnett of Derbyshire, batting here in the one-day international against Sri Lanka at The Oval in 1988, is another player successful in county cricket who failed to make the grade at the highest level.

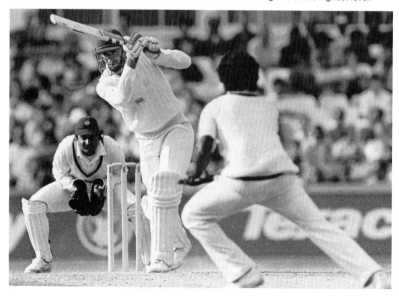

Tony Greig (**left**), and Graham Gooch (**right**) both adopted an upright stance, with the bat raised while waiting for the ball. But while Greig's was a sensible improvisation to compensate for his abnormal height, Gooch's exaggerated stance brought with it problems. Too often he played across the line of the ball.

England recruited me to help some of the England batsmen prepare for the 1990 West Indies tour, and I was happy to do so. But although I was present throughout the series, I was not called upon to help the team in the crucial few days leading up to each Test.

All smiles at Sabina Park: inspecting the pitch before the first Test in the 1990 series with my old adversary Michael Holding **(above)**; and **(right)** Allan Lamb is congratulated by Robin Smith on reaching his magnificent century.

or tea or at close of play, and if they persisted throughout a full day they would be 240 runs adrift.

The fact that this would be rather more than the average batting side might hope to score against them is beside the point. The scale of penalties has to be so great that it will put the game out of reach of the bowling side if they do not get their act together. The object of the exercise is to put an end to what is nothing less than the equivalent of the 'professional foul' in soccer. The West Indies approach denies their opponents a fair crack of the whip. I could field for the West Indies even at the age of fifty, standing at gully or slip and moving every five minutes to a different catching position. To coin a well-worn phrase, it literally is not cricket. Forcing the West Indies to bowl thirty-two overs in two hours would make them use spinners again and improve the level of entertainment.

It would also help if umpires were to be instructed to apply the laws relating to wides strictly. The West Indies bowl a lot of balls, especially down the leg side, that the batsman cannot hope to hit with any certainty. These would be called wide in one-day cricket and I believe they should be called wide in Tests, too. This would put more pressure on the bowlers trying to keep up with the over-rates. Put simply, bowlers should be trying to take wickets and batsmen to score runs, at whatever level they are competing. Right now this is not the case on far too many occasions. When I played Test cricket in the 1960s and 1970s, seventeen and eighteen overs an hour were not unusual, and we should be aiming to get back to those levels. It is hard to believe, but when Australia made 404–3 to beat England at Headingley in 1948 there were 117 overs in the day. England batted on for two runs on the morning of the last day so that they could then use the heaviest roller available in an attempt to break up the pitch, and they subsequently bowled 115 overs at the Australians. Today's England side would easily have prevented the Australians winning by giving them only ninety or so overs. To provide an interesting comparison, Australia got through just eighty-seven overs on the day I completed my hundredth century in the Headingley Test of 1977, sixty-eight of those being bowled by Jeff Thomson, Max Walker and Len Pascoe. The difference of thirty overs says a lot about how attitudes had changed in those thirty-odd years. And nowadays it's become even worse, with ninety or so overs a day being viewed by many as an impossible target!

Viv Richards expressed the view during the 1990 series in the West Indies that it was impossible to average fifteen overs an hour in the tropics because of the heat and the humidity. This was a monstrous statement, which flew in the face of logic. Anyone really interested in finding a solution to this ongoing problem has only to watch the West Indies going about their business in the field. At times they give the distinct impression of being in a trance, becoming energetic only when they are chasing a scoring stroke or trying to convince an umpire with a particularly passionate appeal. They could certainly raise the tempo if they wanted.

Batsmen, too, are guilty of holding up the play these days. I have no argument against short delays to allow a batsman to change his helmet or to receive treatment after being hit on the fingers. I do feel, however, that the game would be speeded up if batsmen coming in were made to cross on the field with those going out, as was the case when I started. These days, especially in Test cricket, you could be forgiven for thinking that the next man in had lost his way somewhere in the pavilion. The batsmen do not even follow the fielding side on to the ground with any sense of purpose after an interval, and many lame excuses are put forward for their leisurely rate of progress.

If my recommendations were adopted no doubt the bowling side would complain about stoppages caused by the batsmen, but the umpires could make due allowance for these, and for interruptions caused by the weather, to make sure that no team was penalized unfairly. Soccer referees add on time for stoppages and for time-wasting and umpires could follow suit. I am aware that Test matches might not last so long, but I am sure that the spectators would much rather see three days of good-quality cricket than four days of desultory action; and a day's play would offer a lot better value for money.

When the International Cricket Conference worked out the scheme to ensure a minimum of ninety overs in a full day, they forgot one important point. In all countries except England the light goes very quickly so only a limited amount of 'extra time' is available at the end of a day. Throughout the 1990 series between England and West Indies both teams knew this full well, so the rule proved impotent. There was not one day in which the full allocation of ninety overs was bowled. Human nature being what it is, players will always look for ways in which to make the system work for them. England were reluctant to bowl more overs, thus giving the West Indians more scoring opportunities, than they received themselves; and every team feels the same. It has become a tit-for-tat situation and cricket is therefore on a downhill spiral.

Even in England the authorities got it wrong when they merely extended the day to accommodate a minimum of ninety overs, for they gave the pacemen plenty of time in which to rest between overs and, indeed, between deliveries. The public like to know the exact hours of play, not what they might be, just as if they go to the cinema they want to know when the film finishes. Realistically, it is a mistake to continue playing at the highest level after 6.30p.m. I understand that in allowing extra time to make up for the weather the Test and County Cricket Board is trying to keep faith with the public, but it is not fair on the players. They have been on the ground, keyed up from around 9.15 or 9.30 in the morning and when it gets to 6.30 they have been at it long enough. When it rains heavily the spectators tend to drift away rather than hang about for hours with nothing much to do. It is much more important to improve the quality of the covering to make sure that there is a prompt resumption whenever the rain stops. Covers generally in England are antiquated, and although there has been some improvement they are still nowhere near good enough.

Whatever regulations are brought in, the pitches on which Test matches are played will always be very important, and there is no doubt in my mind that they have deteriorated alarmingly. In the 1960s, when I began my Test career, the captain who won the toss batted first on most occasions and his success with the coin prompted a good deal of cheering in the dressing-room. The pitches were invariably good unless the weather had seriously affected their preparation and the expectation was that they would eventually take some spin, to make batting more difficult in the later stages. Over the last ten to twelve years, unfortunately, groundsmen have been watering the pitch the day before a game and leaving on more grass, even in the West Indies. They had some marvellous batting strips throughout the Caribbean when I toured in 1968 and 1974, but then decided that their battery of fast bowlers would do better given a bit of help. The position became so serious that the West Indies Board of Control issued a directive before the 1990 series with England, instructing groundsmen to make a big effort to produce better batting conditions. Their concern was not really the good of cricket, but rather that games might finish too early, a trend which could reduce television interest. Sky Television, who paid a lot of money for the right to cover the Tests live, were obviously looking to fill a lot of viewing slots and they would not have been happy with a collection of blank days.

Admittedly there were times in the past when the pitches were too heavily loaded in the batsman's favour, but if groundsmen concentrated on getting them as dry as possible they would turn. To my mind a perfect Test strip is very dry and grassless, offering moderate bounce. A turning pitch is not against the laws of the game and is not unfair, so long as the bounce is consistent. The trouble is that too many groundsmen lack the courage of their convictions and use too much water. As captain I always went out in my spikes to look at the pitch. Quite often when I scraped my foot over an apparently dry surface I found darker-coloured soil underneath. Although many groundsmen stoutly denied watering the pitch, under pressure they finally admitted: 'Well, I did just give it a sprinkling yesterday to help hold it together.' In such conditions the pitch might well get better on the second and third days, so the captain is tempted to play all his quicker bowlers and put the opposition in if he wins the toss. Again the spinner loses out, and the game is less interesting – a bit like chess without, say, the knights or the bishops.

If I were in charge of the England team for a home series with the West Indies I would instruct the groundsmen at the Test centres to prepare grassless, spinning pitches to nullify their fast bowling. I do not see anything wrong with this policy, especially as it would do so much good. Possibly the West Indies would still win, for they are undoubtedly the best team in the world, but they have not enjoyed unlimited success in the one-day competitions, where they do have to maintain a better over-rate, where wides are frequently called for the short ball and where their batsmen have to show a lot of skill against the turning ball. They have not always managed to cope with problems in this direction and were spectacularly defeated by India in Madras in January 1988. The margin was a remarkable 255 runs and Narendra Hirwani, a teenage leg-spinner, had match figures of 16–136, as West Indies were bowled out for 184 and 160. Significantly, off-spinner Arshad Ayub spun the ball like a top, but he took only 1–80, although he bowled forty-two overs. The West Indies are more vulnerable to the ball spinning away from the bat, which is of course more difficult to play than the one spinning in, as the latter can be intercepted with the pad so long as the leg movement is accompanied by the suggestion of a stroke with the bat. The West Indies' management actually protested about the Madras pitch, yet India scored 382 and 217–8 declared and the tourists' complaint rightly got nowhere. They paid the penalty for putting their faith exclusively in pace and lacked the skill to deal with high-class spinners on turning pitches.

I am sure, though, that the spectators enjoyed the match, just as the Australians did at Sydney a year later, when the West Indies were again confounded on a slow, turning pitch. On that occasion, Australian captain Border, who had taken only sixteen wickets in his previous hundred Tests, finished with 11–96. With his slow left-arm he turned the ball away from the bat and Australia won by seven wickets. It has to be said that Border claimed four of his seven first-innings wickets with rank long hops and the West Indies simply 'gave up the ghost'. Even so, the two sides produced a very entertaining contest, Australia scoring 401 and 82–3 in reply to 224 and 256. My good friend Desmond Haynes scored 143 in the West Indies' second innings and David Boon hit 149 in Australia's first, so no-one could argue that the pitch was not good enough. What it did do was to switch the emphasis from sheer pace and bring a breath of fresh air into international cricket.

In addition to getting the playing conditions right, the legislators should also address themselves to the growing problem of arguments about umpires in Test cricket. Hardly a series goes by anywhere in the world without some complaint from the visiting team, and Pakistan's captain Imran Khan is not the only influential figure to press for neutral umpires. I have supported such a move for a long time. Umpires will never be perfect, for they are human and make mistakes, as they did in the 1987 World Cup in India, but because these umpires were neutral everyone accepted the rough with the smooth. There were no serious complaints and the same applied when John Hampshire and John Holder, who are on the Test and County Cricket Board panel, went out from England to officiate in the 1990 series between Pakistan and India. Both sides recognized their impartiality, while Hampshire and Holder for their part operated without undue pressure, knowing that they would not be accused of home bias. The introduction of neutral umpires would also prevent the unpleasant tit-for-tat atmosphere which has grown up between English and Pakistani officials and players. Pakistan objected to David Constant and Ken Palmer when they toured over here in 1987, asking that they should both be removed from the Test panel. Imran indicated that he and his team had no faith in Constant, following his performance in the 1982 Headingley Test. The Test and County Cricket Board, however, stood by Constant and Palmer. Constant umpired at Lord's in the second Test, Palmer at Leeds in the third, and the two of them together in the fifth and final Test at the Oval. England, in turn, objected to Shakeel Khan when they visited Pakistan the following winter, but were predictably ignored. The England tourists were even more unhappy when they discovered that Shakoor Rana had been appointed for the second Test, for he had already established a reputation for upsetting visiting teams. In Karachi in the winter of 1984–5 New Zealand was led off the field by their captain Jeremy Coney as an act of protest against Shakoor's attitude. All this led to the dreadful scenes involving Mike Gatting, a truly international incident that could have been avoided had everyone agreed beforehand to neutral umpires.

In 1982 English officials had been in a difficult situation when the Indians objected to Constant. The Test and County Cricket Board withdrew him then, and although his match fee was paid, however diplomatically the Board wrapped up its action, it suggested a lack of confidence in a senior umpire. The Board was seen by many to be bowing to pressure, which is probably why it reacted differently by backing Constant and Palmer in 1987 and why the Pakistanis took their matching stance. As I see it, the International Cricket Conference could establish the umpiring pattern when they draw up the forthcoming international fixtures, giving all concerned plenty of time to respond by selecting and preparing the probable match officials. A series between Australia and India might well have three English umpires to work on a rota basis throughout the Tests and, similarly, a series involving England and West Indies might have three Indian umpires. I believe that the umpires should all be from the same country because they would be required to spend a lot of time together, making cultural familiarity important. The Test umpires could perhaps officiate in one first-class game beforehand to 'get the feel of things', but they would subsequently stand only in the Tests, resting between the big matches, and with three of them they should avoid becoming stale or tired. Obviously extra money would have to be found to fund the scheme, but Test cricket keeps the game going worldwide and it is important to get things absolutely right at the top with, if necessary, the assistance of sponsorship.

Firm, independent umpiring would also help to reduce the rash of bad behaviour that has crept into cricket, dissent becoming almost commonplace in some instances. I very much regret that England has a poor record, with Chris Broad fanning the flames of discord in Pakistan before Mike Gatting and Shakoor Rana indulged in their slanging match. More recently, Nasser Hussain revealed his lack of maturity almost as soon as England's 1990 tour to the West Indies got under way, twice challenging an umpire's decision.

There have been many other serious outbreaks of trouble, including a physical confrontation between Dennis Lillee and Pakistan batsman Javed Miandad, Lillee's aluminium bat tantrum and, more recently, the Pakistan team walking off during their match against Victoria early in 1990. Such actions would have been unthinkable in the 1960s, when I began. When a decision went against you or your team you just carried on, expressing your displeasure by, for example, not applauding a batsman who got runs after failing to walk. The England team did that to Eddie Barlow in Cape Town in 1965, but nobody said anything, nor did they attempt to pressure the umpire.

I must admit that I ran into trouble on Mike Brearley's tour to Australia in 1978–9, calling umpire Don Weser 'a cheat'. I reacted after he had turned down two apparently plumb lbw shouts by Ian Botham against Kim Hughes, who was hit low down in front of the middle stump as he played back in each case. My only excuse was that I had been badly upset by losing the captaincy of Yorkshire in appallingly spiteful circumstances following the death of my mother. Tour manager Doug Insole showed a lot of understanding and I had the courage to say sorry to the umpire afterwards. I knew that what I had done in the heat of the moment was wrong. Unfortunately many of those who offend today are convinced they are right. In the circumstances, I was interested to hear Stanley Matthews talking on his seventy-fifth birthday. The soccer maestro, discussing behaviour, said that in his day if a footballer was sent off while playing for England he was very unlikely to be selected for his country again. Soccer and rugby referees, of course, have the power to dismiss a player for breaking the laws of the game, but the poor cricket umpire is ill-equipped to deal with offenders. He is, in effect, a eunuch, unable to order a player to the dressing-room. I feel cricket could learn a lot about discipline from other sports.

In soccer, referees have a wide range of disciplinary action at their disposal. At the bottom end of the scale there is the free kick, with the yellow card for a caution and the red card for dismissal. Cricket, of course, would need a different system and could adopt something similar to tennis. Match officials can hand out penalty points for persistent misconduct such as shouting, swearing and arguing with line calls, as well as throwing rackets petulantly. John McEnroe was ruled out of the Australian Open in 1990 when he refused to accept an umpire's authority.

The need for umpires to be handed extra authority was underlined during the England series in the West Indies in 1990. The antics of Viv Richards, in particular, were unacceptable. He argued that his frantic dancing and exaggerated celebrations of a bowling success for his side – real or imagined – were a natural expression of his feelings. This might well have been the case, but if it was, then he must learn to exercise greater self-control. Such behaviour puts the umpire under intolerable pressure; as bowlers like Dennis Lillee, Ian Botham and Richard Hadlee have done in the past when they turned to make an lbw appeal with both forefingers raised.

Cricket cannot afford to let things drift. The players who continue to step out of line must be hit hard, and so must the team for which they play. I would suggest a penalty system with, for example, one point being awarded against a batsman, bowler or fielder for dissent. The more serious cases, such as a prolonged refusal to leave the field or the smashing of the stumps with the bat, would merit two penalty points. Players should also be punished for what the Australians call 'sledging', the practice of constantly trying to upset the batsman with bad language and a barrage of sneering. Australian 'macho man' Merv Hughes is a notable offender, who upset Pakistan captain Imran Khan during the 1990 series. The umpires attracted some criticism for not taking action, but apart from a hard word there was not much they could do. With recourse to penalty points the umpires could soon settle any disputes, and exert more control on the field. Once a player had reached three penalty points he would automatically be suspended from the next match, while a six-point tally would cost him three matches. To give the offender an incentive to mend his ways, any penalty points could be removed from his record after, say, three clear years, thus wiping the slate clean.

Some of my suggestions no doubt seem revolutionary, but cricket must move with the times. Declining standards of behaviour in the game reflect life in the outside world and the legislators cannot afford to live in the past. I believe that one of the biggest changes to come in the next few years will be the introduction of night Test cricket in Australia. Delaying the start makes a lot of sense with their climate, for I am sure spectators would be attracted by the possibility of play going on until 9.30p.m. With a 2.30 start, tea could be taken at 4.30 and dinner at 6.50, leaving a last session to get under way at 7.30. Those hours would make it possible for people to attend on their way home from work, with admission prices reduced to two-thirds for the second and third sessions and half for the last two hours. Kerry Packer used a similar system to good effect in his World Series matches.

I also expect the authorities to do away with the rest day during Tests because it is unnecessary so long as players can take a good break before the games start. There should be at least two clear days before each Test. The authorities have got things the wrong way round in timing the Tests. They rush players from county games more or less straight into these important matches and then give them a meaningless day off in the middle. The rest day is little more than a waste of time because the players are hanging about while remaining tense about the state of the game, so they cannot relax. Sooner or later, those in charge ought to accept that a better-balanced programme would provide the players with the opportunity to recover mentally as well as physically from the rigours of their normal county routine.

There is so much that can be done to make Test cricket a more attractive product. It only needs courage, enterprise and imagination – qualities which so far have been lacking in the seven countries which make up the International Cricket Conference.

6

That man Botham

Shortly before 6.30p.m. on the cold, cheerless evening of 28 April 1984, I played an amazingly careless stroke that cost me my wicket. The occasion was the opening championship match of the season between Somerset and Yorkshire at Taunton and this rare lapse was to a long hop by Ian Botham which I obligingly hooked down the throat of Mark Davis at long leg. In every other circumstance I would certainly have negotiated a fairly harmless delivery comfortably enough, for I had made only 6 and was really looking to play out time after a hard day in the field. For most of his career Botham had this strange ability to pick up wickets with bad balls, to persuade batsmen to sacrifice themselves as though hypnotized. Perhaps it had something to do with his own lemming-like aptitude for self-destruction, for his success with the most ordinary deliveries defied logic.

Botham made his England début against the Australians in the 1977 Trent Bridge Test which also marked my return to Test cricket after a three-year absence, and he looked out of his depth in his opening spell. He came back in the afternoon, however, to produce the first of his remarkable bursts – 4–13 in thirty-four balls. The delivery that began it all was nothing more than a gentle loosener, well short of a length, but Greg Chappell, aiming a fierce drive, played on. Like me at Taunton, the Australian captain could hardly believe what he had done. More recently, Botham had a mesmeric effect on the 1986 New Zealand tourists. His absence from all but the last Test of a depressing summer, in which India and New Zealand both defeated England in a three-match series, was because of his suspension from 29 May to 31 July. This followed his admission that he had used cannabis and his making comments in public without the approval of his county. His eagerly awaited return came at the Oval, where New Zealand opener Bruce Edgar gently steered his first ball, a fairly tame delivery, to slip.

No author creating a work of fiction would have dared to write either that little scene or to recount many of Botham's other great moments, because few of them seem credible in print. In August, after serving his suspension, he presented the Leukaemia Research Fund with a cheque for £880,000, the proceeds from his great charity walk from John o'Groats to Land's End. He is a truly incredible man, complex, naïve, difficult, brilliant, foolish, loyal and aggressive in turn. His record is phenomenal, highlighted by dazzling feats with both bat and ball. At Lord's in 1978 he became the first Test match player to score a century (108) and take eight wickets in an innings (for 34), Pakistan being his helpless victims. He completed the double of 1,000 runs and 100 wickets in the fewest number of Tests – twenty-one – and in 1982 he struck the bemused Indians for 208 from 219 balls, probably the fastest double century of all time in terms of balls faced.

I hit my ninety-eighth first-class century in the Nottingham Test that brought Botham on to the international stage, so we are clearly representatives of totally different generations, but I think that I have played close enough with him to recognize his strengths and weaknesses on and off the field. I have had the opportunity to study him at close quarters, both as his England captain, and later under his Test match leadership. I can claim just a little bit of credit for developing Botham's Test career, for, surprising though it may seem at this distance, Mike Brearley did not pick him for any of the three Tests in Pakistan during the 1977–8 tour. The hard, crusty pitches persuaded him to rely largely on spin. Brearley broke his arm fending off a delivery from the fast-medium Sikander Bakht in a one-day fixture against Sind at Karachi shortly before the third Test and, having taken over then, I led the side in three Tests against New Zealand, bringing Botham into the team.

He did little in the first Test at Wellington, where the home side recorded their first victory over England in forty-eight attempts, but he fully justified my faith in him at Christchurch, hitting one 6 and twelve 4s in his maiden Test century and claiming 8–111 with the ball. It was a clear foretaste of things to come and I recognized from the start that he was an exceptionally gifted player. In world terms, he probably stands second behind Garfield Sobers as the best allrounder of modern times and I cannot pay him any greater compliment than that. At his best he is an exceptionally aggressive fast-medium bowler, who could swing the ball prodigiously at times, while his batting, like his personality, reflected his extrovert approach to life. In addition, he ranks as one of the best slip fielders, with a wonderfully gifted pair of hands. He is an imposing figure, constantly chasing rainbows. He wants to do everything in life, to climb mountains, fly aeroplanes, play football for England and make the impossible at cricket look commonplace. I think he would probably have been better had he played cricket fifty years earlier, when the game was not quite so professional, when the more Corinthian attitude was encouraged. He might then have combined football and cricket at the highest level. I tend to think of him as a bit like Biggles, the story-book hero of the immediate post-War years, because Botham likes the idea of coming to people's rescue and displaying both his strength and his courage. He is in fact very brave and throughout his career he has reacted positively, if not always wisely, to situations. He simply cannot stand aside or walk away from trouble and is always ready to meet it more than halfway, which is why at a very early age he gained a reputation as a 'hell-raiser'. Many of the tales, of course, have grown with the telling, as they did about Fred Trueman, and Botham has been happy to live with the exaggerations because he regards himself as being a bit larger than life.

He is also the victim of selective amnesia and forgets all the embarrassing things that he has done or said, assuming that he can bluster his way out of any situation. Take the business to do with South Africa when a group of us went out there in 1982, defying political pressure to exercise our right to earn a living. Botham came back from the tour of India, which preceded this unofficial visit, saying that he could not have looked his great friend Viv Richards in the eye if he had accepted an offer to join us. The players who were with him in India, however, knew that was just fantasy because he had attended all the meetings at which South Africa was discussed. Then, in January 1990, it was reported that he had again been prepared to go there with Mike Gatting's rebel squad, pulling out of the negotiations only when the organizers either couldn't or wouldn't meet his demand for a £600,000 fee. Newspaper reports indicated that Botham had spoken to Richards about playing in South Africa and been told that the West Indian captain would not criticize him for making the trip. His solicitor, Alan Herd, was quoted as saying: 'A major point for Ian was that if he had gone, it could have ended his Test career and could well have meant the loss of future contracts in the United Kingdom.' It is not easy to understand or accept at face value his change of attitude, particularly as he approached me in 1981, when, remember, he was England captain, to talk about South Africa. We were in Barbados, having just got there after leaving Guyana, and, with one Test having been called off for political reasons, we had plenty of time on our hands. We were not, in fact, sure that the tour would continue, as another island was having second thoughts about allowing us to enter with Robin Jackman, who had strong South African connections, in the party. On that occasion there was no mention of Richards or morality. The subject of the conversation was money. He has shut this out of his mind, and there is no doubt that he has reshaped the course of events in other areas too to suit his convenience.

There is, for instance, the story of how he ran me out in the second Test against New Zealand in 1978. The version that has gained most credibility over the years is that Botham deliberately left me stranded to hurry along the declaration, which he thought might be delayed so long as I remained at the crease. I suppose that could have been the case, although he was only in his sixth Test at the time he owed his place in the team to me, and my dismissal had no effect one way or the other on the declaration. I was clear in my own mind that I intended to leave the bowlers a full day in which to bowl out New Zealand, which is exactly what I did and England ended up winning by 174 runs. There is, though, rather more substance to the legend that has grown up around Botham's confrontation with Ian Chappell in the winter of 1976–7, when he went out to Australia with Yorkshire's Graham Stevenson on a Whitbread Scholarship scheme. Botham was no more than an up-and-coming prospect at the time, although word had already got around the first-class circuit in England that here was a youngster with a lot of ability and confidence. He and Stevenson had been practising with the Victoria first team in Melbourne, and naturally mingled with the home players when they went along to the bar for a drink later. Chappell had just retired, but he still took an active interest in cricket. He arrived on the scene and immediately started to have a go at 'the poms', trying to wind Botham up. As Stevenson says, Botham 'politely asked' Chappell to go away and leave him alone, but this request was ignored. Inevitably Botham reacted, grabbing Chappell, shaking him and pushing him down the bar, breaking a few glasses in the process. If Botham hit Chappell, I believe it was largely by accident when he got hold of him, but he certainly picked up a bottle and adopted a threatening attitude before the other customers stepped in to restore the peace. Significantly, a lot of the Victorian players defended Botham, who definitely did not forget the incident.

The two came face-to-face again in Adelaide on 5 December 1979 during England's winter tour of Australia, when Chappell had emerged from retirement to try to regain his Test place. He was making his first appearance for South Australia after a three-week suspension for using bad language to an umpire. Throughout the match Chappell subjected us to a stream of critical comment and I batted through a lot of it as I scored my 117th century to equal the total of the great Sir Donald Bradman on his home ground. That was a proud moment for me so I ignored Chappell's boorish behaviour, but word of what was going on filtered back to the dressing-room and Botham could hardly wait to get at him on the second day of the match. He greeted Chappell's arrival in the middle by going round the wicket and digging the ball in short. Chappell gloved a nasty lifter down to third man for a single and was very annoyed when the umpire signalled a leg bye, turning his attention to the unfortunate official. Chappell had a very rough time as Botham peppered him, and he almost sat on his stumps before edging a catch to David Bairstow for nought.

One of Botham's weaknesses has been the way in which he lets things get out of hand. He can, for example, be very funny and he has a marvellous sense of humour, but he can also be a bully. I have often found myself the subject of his mickey-taking; when we played for England together he would mess about in the dressing-room, playing defensively to imaginary balls and mocking me by saying 'I just can't get this left knee in the right place' as he contorted his leg into ridiculous positions. He often taunted me about his extra strength, offering me his bat and suggesting: 'Get a bat like this, Fiery, and then you might get it off the square,' and people who did not know us might have thought that he was against me.

This was not the case, however, and when he was England captain he would tell me 'Get down to fine leg and entertain your fans.' Equally, he always left me alone when I was getting ready to bat. Just before I went out, he would quietly whisper: 'You stay in all day, Fiery. Wear the bowlers down. Then I'll come in after tea and slog them all over the field when they're tired and bored to death.' Botham could be very quickwitted, too. I recall on one occasion during the 1978–9 series in Australia Rodney Hogg, who sometimes lost his balance a bit in the delivery stride, stretching himself full length on the pitch after letting the ball go. Botham stood back as it passed safely wide and then said: 'I know you think I'm great, Hoggy, but there's no need to go down on your hands and knees to me in public.'

All the same, I did not christen him Guy the Gorilla for nothing, and there have been occasions when he has overstepped the mark. A couple of examples will show what I mean. In November 1979 we were travelling back to our Sydney hotel from Newcastle after a one-day game against Northern New South Wales. Botham persuaded two of the other players to grab my arms and pin them behind the seat. He then squirted me with a water-pistol and jokingly accused me of taking all the balls from leg-spinner Kerry O'Keeffe and not allowing Wayne Larkins to get down to that end. All this was fair enough, but gradually Botham became more boisterous, pulling off my shirt, trousers and underpants. He put on my underpants over his trousers and covered me with shaving foam, literally from head to toe, so that I resembled Father Christmas. He refused for a long time to give me back my underpants or trousers. They eventually let me go and I cleaned myself up a bit with cotton wool and a handkerchief from one of the lads, but I spent the rest of the journey with my arms aching, sitting naked in my shoes and socks.

In the end, as we approached the hotel, I put on my jacket and Elton John cap and threatened to get off the bus just as I was, which merely provoked howls of mirth from Botham and the rest of the team. Tour manager Alec Bedser at last managed to find my underpants and trousers so that I was properly dressed when I left the coach and Mike Brearley, the captain, said: 'You did really well not to lose your temper. There was a lot going on then.' Botham undoubtedly sees himself as the leader of the pack, but he actually resents being called a bully. I took exception to his antics in the West Indies in 1981, when he was captain. We were in the team-room after returning from the one-day international in Guyana on 26 February. Botham called us together to tell us about the Jackman situation. The Surrey seamer's arrival as replacement for the unfit Bob Willis made us unwelcome in Guyana, and Botham said we would be leaving. We had to hang about for a couple of hours until Alan Smith, the manager, turned up to tell us much the same thing, so we were all fed up and bored. It was unbearably hot in the team-room, and a few people were drinking wine to ease the tension and pass the time. I was lying on the floor, resting my back, when Botham said something provocative. I replied in kind. He jumped on top of me, pinned my arms back and started drumming with his fingers quite hard on my forehead, which hurt. I said: 'Get off. If you don't get your own way or somebody disagrees with what you say, you just try to bully them.' He carried on and tried to make light of his actions: 'It'll start to hurt soon, Fiery. The pain will dig deep into your subconscious.' I said: 'It already does hurt, and I repeat that you are a bully. I'm convinced of that now.' I could see that I had got through to him and he did not like it, although he did not know how to give up without losing face.

There was a sequel in the VIP lounge at the airport as we were leaving Guyana on 27 February. We had snatched a snack with some Coke or beer and I was using one of my toothpicks. Botham, sitting a few yards away, asked if he could have one and I said that I gave them only to my friends. He looked at me and shrugged. He did not say anything, but he got the message very clearly.

The other side of Botham's nature had become clear in Trinidad during the first Test, when he was larking about around the swimming-pool at the team's hotel. He decided it was very amusing to go around pulling down people's shorts, but as the afternoon wore on his antics took on a violent undertone. Eventually Peter Willey, who is a very tough customer from the North-east, had had enough, so he threw some of Botham's gear into the pool. 'Hey, that's mine,' snapped Botham. 'I know,' said Willey; 'what are you going to do about it?' Guessing that Willey meant business, Botham avoided a head-on confrontation. That represented one of the few occasions when he dodged trouble.

Behind all the bluster, however, Botham has a keen mind and he knows a lot about cricket. When there is nobody about and he does not feel he has to live up to his reputation he will talk sensibly about tactics. He can be pretty shrewd, too. He showed a lot of imagination at Lord's in 1981, during the second Test of the West Indies tour. We had been bowled out for 269 on a very flat pitch and they took full advantage of the situation. On the Saturday we were taking a pounding in the field, with Desmond Haynes on his way to 184 and Viv Richards racing to 145. The total went past 200 with only one wicket down. Suddenly Botham said to me: 'Come on, Fiery, you have a bowl.' I kept walking towards fine leg. I thought, I am not hearing this. Botham shouted after me: 'Come on, bowl.' 'Are you joking?' I asked. 'No, definitely not,' he replied. 'Well, you ought to be,' I said. 'Have you seen the score?' 'Never mind that,' insisted Botham, 'They'll be terrified of you.' 'They'll not be half as terrified as me,' I exclaimed. All this went on in the middle of the wicket and I felt it was crazy, so I decided to turn my cap round and bowl with the neb at the back. I was ready to try anything to distract the batsmen. 'I don't know what you expect me to do when all the bowlers have failed,' I protested. I had to laugh, because I bowled a very tidy over, the first maiden to Haynes for a long, long time. 'Try another,' ordered Botham cheerfully, although I did not think I could get away with it twice. Botham said: 'I have just heard Desmond saying to Viv that he'd like to change ends because he's worried that you're going to get him out. Viv said he was happy where he was.' Neither of them wanted to face me just in case I did get a wicket and I did my best to build up the tension. Desmond is a very good friend of mine and he did not dare look at me, playing so far forward that he almost trod on my foot. After each delivery he gazed studiously at the ground and when he did get to my end I told him that if I did get him out I would never let him forget it. He replied: 'No way. I'm taking good care you don't get me out.' I got through seven overs for 11 runs and that little spell proved that Botham had some insight into the finer points.

I thought, though, that when he got the England captaincy in 1980, aged twenty-five, he was too young, too inexperienced. To me at the time he was too much one of the lads. He wanted to live his own life fully without trying to get involved in sorting out other people's problems. I told him that it would have been better if he had shouldered the burden of captaincy towards the end of his career. I understood his ambition and most youngsters coming into first-class cricket dream of being captain of England, but Botham took charge at a very difficult time in a home series against West Indies. They were easily the strongest team in the world, with probably the greatest quartet of fast bowlers the world has ever seen. Botham would strenuously deny that he found it difficult to cope with responsibility because he never thought there was anything in life he could not do. In one way that is his great strength, but it is also his Achilles' heel. He cannot see any pitfalls and he never sees anything wrong in what he has done. Incredibly, therefore, when we got to the fourth and final Test of the 1981 West Indies tour at Kingston, Jamaica, Botham informed us all at the team meeting: 'I'm very pleased with the way we've played against this lot, so let's give a good account of ourselves in this last one.' I was staggered at the way he tried to gloss over the fact that we had not really played to our full ability, losing the Test in Trinidad by an innings and 79 runs and the one in Barbados by 298 runs. Perhaps, to an extent, Botham was demonstrating his loyalty to the players, which was unswerving.

He defended me from potential criticism after the Centenary Test against Australia at Lord's in August 1980. Greg Chappell set England a target of 370 on the last day, so to win we would have had to score at a run a minute for over six hours. This was never on, and Botham told me: 'One or two of us are not in all that much form, Fiery, so stay in and make sure we don't lose.' His caution was justified by the fact that England's last seven wickets in the first innings had crashed for 68, but nevertheless some members of the press came round to see if there was a story to be concocted about me playing for myself. Botham did not flinch from the responsibility of his decision. I have known those who did change their minds in public, especially when the player concerned was not present to defend himself, but Botham said quite clearly that I had played extremely well and had followed his instructions to the letter.

He also supported me in January 1979 over an incident in Australia involving Tony Francis, a representative of ITN, who I felt had let me down very badly. I had been troubled with neck and hand injuries and could not play in the two Benson and Hedges World Series Cup games leading up to the finals, although I was being pressed to hurry the recovery process to play against West Indies in Melbourne. I felt very down at the time, particularly as some people on the tour committee had been saying things about me off the record to the press, expressing opinions that could do nothing but harm. They had not actually said I was fit and did not want to play, but nor had they said I was unfit and unable to play. They just dropped hints and made it look bad for me. Francis rang up from Sydney and said that the ITV crew were doing little snippets of the cricket for the news bulletins. I had got on with him pretty well and he gave me the clear impression that his was mainly a social call. He asked how I was and I told him I was a bit depressed because my hand was still painful.

I added that I was worried that I would not get any runs when the best-of-three finals began in Sydney next day and that I would buy him a bottle of champagne if I got 50. He said he would buy me one if I didn't – 'to drown your sorrows'. It all remained very light-hearted and casual and he said: 'I've just got to do a piece on the match and I'm really ringing up to see if you'll be playing.' I remember he rang about 1.00p.m. and the selectors were meeting as we spoke. 'You can ring Alec Bedser at about two-thirty and he'll tell you,' I informed Francis, adding: 'I'm sure they'll pick me because the way they've been talking they'll pick me if I have to play on one leg. They've been going on about me when I haven't played and I've got to get fit to play now even if I'm not a hundred per cent.' I told him how I felt because he had to do a quick report to London and it seemed reasonable to inform him of the position on a friendly basis so that he understood the background. I was horrified to discover that my remarks, some taken out of context, had been turned into a sensational *Sunday Telegraph* story in which I was shown as being critical of the England captain, Mike Brearley, and suggesting that I wanted to go home. To make matters worse, as we flew to Sydney, a couple of the team, half-joking, half-sarcastic, asked: 'Are you going home or what, Fiery?' Bedser called a meeting with Brearley and me to sort things out and Francis rang me about lunchtime to say he'd had a call from the captain, who had been very angry about the newspaper article. Francis admitted that he had written it, but claimed that it was honest journalism. I told him that I had treated him as a friend and that what I had said was confidential. I believed him to be entirely concerned with television. Otherwise I would have treated him far more cautiously.

The sequel was that Brearley withdrew team co-operation with Francis and, when Botham took over, he followed the same hard line. Francis protested strongly, calling in his editor and the Test and County Cricket Board public relations man Peter Lush became involved. Botham stuck to his guns, though. I very much appreciated Botham's attitude and I would really have liked to help him during the trip to the Caribbean, but there were two obstacles. In the first place Botham did not seem to want any advice from me and, in any case, England appointed Geoff Miller, of Derbyshire, as vice-captain ahead of me when the original choice, Bob Willis, returned home due to injury. That decision inevitably undermined the team's prospects. Tour manager Alan Smith hesitantly outlined the position to me in my room in Guyana. I was absolutely shattered. I did not say anything and he did not offer any explanation. I tried to reason out how Miller, with his limited experience, could help Ian with tactics. The only other player with any knowledge of West Indian conditions was Chris Old, who had toured in 1974, so I had felt sure that Botham would want to lean on me for the benefit of the team. Any success the team enjoyed would be to his credit at Lord's, and I had always got on well with him. In fact, Miller's promotion gave Botham the opportunity to dominate. He apparently did not want a vice-captain who might challenge his opinions. Several players, including Willey and Stevenson, approached me to say they had had enough of Botham, who would not listen to anyone. David Bairstow argued that Botham resented anyone who might just edge him out of the limelight: he could never stand anyone being more popular than he was.

Bairstow may well have been very close to the mark, for when Botham had gone off injured at Headingley in the

1980 Test against the West Indies I took charge, bringing on Graham Gooch to bowl straight away, and he took a couple of wickets. The press made a fuss, highlighting my decision as a master-stroke, and I suppose Botham hated that. Presumably he saw me as a threat and wanted to keep me away from the centre of power. The weakness of having Miller as vice-captain was exposed when he failed to earn selection for the last three Tests. After I had been dismissed in the Barbados Test I sat with Botham in the players' enclosure and asked him how things stood.

Gooch and Botham had already clashed in a row sparked when Botham had said that he did not want players training by running on the beach on the morning of a match, adding: 'That particularly applies to you, Goochie.' Gooch hit the roof. 'I don't accept that. What I do to get fit is my own affair. Provided I perform on the field that's all that matters,' he insisted. Botham developed the argument. 'You complained in Tuesday's practice match that you were tired,' he pointed out. 'You complained when you were batting that you were tired.' Gooch said that he had bowled ten or twelve overs and made 84 runs and was entitled to be tired. Botham made the point that Gooch had said he was tired at the start of his innings. Gooch responded by saying: 'You should look at your own affairs before accusing anyone else of doing something wrong. You don't practise properly. You go in the nets and slog it around, so you don't set a good example. I don't see you doing any exercises at all.' Botham hit back with the remark that a batsman who had made only one Test century could hardly talk about batting. That was a bit below the belt; ironically, Gooch went on to score 116 in the Barbados Test. As the heated discussion went backwards and forwards, the manager went over to try to catch Botham's eye and lower the temperature. Smith tried to gloss over the exchanges by saying: 'Now then, lads, it has been a very full and frank discussion and I have been very interested listening. I think the captain has been very brave to ask everyone to have their say and, after all, he is very young and inexperienced, so we must give him all the help and support we can.' No doubt if I had been captain I would have been crucified for belittling one of my best players in front of the rest of the squad.

Despite everything, I remained keen to help, so, as we talked in Barbados, I asked Botham whether Gooch would now be in charge if he had to leave the field. 'I saw him talking to the bowlers a lot on the first day,' I said. I wondered if he had been awarded the 'silent stripes' to give him seniority in an emergency. 'No,' said Botham, 'if I go off you're in charge. Gooch wasn't told to talk to the bowlers. I think he was just trying to get Graham Dilley to bowl a bit quicker.' I asked him why he had accepted Miller as vice-captain and not used me a bit more. 'I was outvoted on Miller by six to one,' he told me. 'The selectors had a chat in England and when they spoke to me on the telephone it was all cut and dried. The first words Bedser spoke to me on the subject were: "You don't want Boycott, do you?"' Botham claimed that he had argued he could do a lot worse than have me as his vice-captain, but added: 'Alec then said it was out of the question.' Bedser might have said that, but then again it might have been another attack of 'selective amnesia' on Botham's part. He admitted that Gooch was fed up and ready for home and that Willis did not want me in a position of authority as captain or vice-captain. I found myself quite confused. I knew that Botham had first asked Gooch if he would accept the vice-captaincy were it offered, so why had he discussed me with Bedser?

Botham went on to say that he would have preferred me or Gooch and claimed that he had told Bedser he wanted someone with a secure place in the team, but that he had been simply outvoted. Botham discussed a few points about England's approach and sought my views on moving Gooch down the order with Bill Athey opening, but generally he did not seek my advice.

For example, during the 1979–80 tour to Australia he was batting very poorly and it was not easy for him to regain his form. The Australians had the Packer players available again for the Benson and Hedges World Series and the West Indies were formidable as ever. Botham continually got out 1bw through shuffling across the crease, rather than going forward or back, and playing across the line.

Balls that Botham believed were going well down the leg side were actually hitting middle and, as I watched his confusion grow, he asked everyone in the team except me what he was doing wrong. I got on with my own job, reasoning that sooner or later he would see sense and come to me, but things got worse and still he did not say a word. January arrived and Botham was bemoaning his lack of form with the bat as we were sitting in the dressing-room at Sydney, when I could stand it no longer. 'I can tell you what's wrong. It's quite simple,' I told him. There was silence around the dressing-room for a second or two before he gave me his full attention. I explained about his foot movement and suggested that he should move forward and back instead of across. The transformation came about immediately. In the Melbourne Test he reached a century in exactly two hundred minutes, going on to make 119 not out. Then, in the Jubilee Test against India in Bombay on our way home, he top-scored with 114, in addition to taking 13–106; but he never said thank you and he never mentioned the incident again. I suppose the truth is that he has never given a lot of thought to his own game, relying entirely on his huge reservoir of natural talent, which is why I think his best days are long behind him. Indeed, if he is not careful he will go downhill quickly and tarnish his image as a genuinely great allround cricketer. He has retained the ability to make money, but the years of rich living, of burning the candle at both ends, have taken their toll and it is a struggle for him as he moves towards the close of his career with Worcestershire. I bumped into Mike Brearley at the Oval Test in 1989 and, as we discussed the future for England, he put forward the theory that Botham might remain a central figure as a batsman who bowled a bit to supplement the attack. I could not agree, because I do not believe that he can change his attitude to batting at this late stage.

The one flaw in Botham's remarkable record is a miserable average of 21.03, with a highest score of 81, from thirty-six Test innings against the West Indies. My explanation for his failure against the best team he has faced is that they always carried too much fire-power. It is impossible to tackle four very fast bowlers head on and win. A batsman has to use his brains and put the emphasis on technique to survive. He must wear them down, like a boxer does his opponent. I recall seeing Muhammad Ali on the Terry Wogan show with a galaxy of boxing stars, including George Foreman and Joe Frazier. When Wogan inquired how Ali would have tackled the mighty Mike Tyson, then unbeaten heavyweight champion of the world, he said without hesitation: 'Stick and run, man.' There is no shame in backing off and using your head when the opposition has an obvious strength, but Botham finds it difficult to think his way through a situation. In 1981 we were batting together during the first Test in Trinidad. 'If we lose this Test, heads will roll,' Botham had said before the innings began. We were the last effective partnership with the new ball due. 'Don't do anything silly,' I said to him shortly after he arrived in the middle. 'The law of averages indicates that they will probably get one of us with the new ball, but we simply cannot afford to lose both our wickets. One of us should stick around to hold the tail-enders together. If we can do that we may just have a chance of saving the game.' Botham nodded his agreement – and then within minutes slogged at Richards' gentle off-spin to get out, caught in the deep! He also attempted to attack the West Indies' pacemen in 1986 under David Gower and again he came off second best.

He was like that from the start of his career. He was obviously still feeling his way when I picked him for the first Test in Wellington in 1978. I put him down at seven in the batting order for a match that was played in a gale force wind, the strongest I have experienced in my life. Chris Old bowled superbly into it for England, but Richard Hadlee was a lot more dangerous with the elements at his back and the ball whizzed through like a tracer bullet. Even so, Botham went out and tried to hook virtually every delivery. The pitch had some limitations and it was going to be the last Test there for three years because they went on to develop the ground, but Botham went on hooking away until he holed out to square leg. 'You dozy so-and-so,' I said when he arrived back in the pavilion, but he only shrugged and replied: 'I wanted to hit him.'

When playing fast bowlers he should have been more patient, curbing his aggressive instincts. If he had concentrated on occupying the crease, then there would have been times when, with the bowlers tired, he could have dominated – but his outlook lets him down. He had a technical fault, too, against pace; he always stood too far away from the vulnerable area around his off stump. Great batsmen do not give the bowlers much sight of the stumps.

Not all of them stand in the same position, of course, but they all move back, across and in to the stumps just before the bowler lets go of the ball. Thus they limit the bowler's view of his target and get their eyes in line with the offstump. Botham is not a good back-foot defensive player; he has never needed to be as he attacked anything short from bowlers up to fast-medium. He attempted to pull, cut or hook from the start. Bowlers with real pace do not allow the batsman to play these strokes for very long, so Botham's inability to get back on the defensive has been his undoing against the West Indies.

Even when he was trying to regain his England place against the 1989 Australians, Botham could not settle down to the hard work of establishing an innings. Botham played against Yorkshire in the Sunday League at Scarborough on 16 July 1989, when I provided some expert comments for Yorkshire Television. When Botham was batting, I leaned from the commentary box and jokingly indicated that he should be playing straight rather than across the line, and his response was to try to hit me with some lofted drives! Later I went into the Worcestershire dressing-room and we had a long chat, during the course of which I stressed that he had to alter his approach if he wanted to extend his international career as a batsman. I argued that future Test demands on him would be different, because he no longer had two strings to his bow. In the past he had been able to bat with a lot of freedom, safe in the knowledge that if he failed his bowling would still guarantee his selection. I tried to help by telling him that he could not just play steadily for 10 or 15 runs and then have a 'dart'. I emphasized the virtues of prolonging his concentration to take him through to 50 or 60 and, perhaps 100. Ray Illingworth used Basil D'Oliveira as a main number five batsman who could chip in with little seamers at the right time. He should have been Botham's role-model and that is the point I tried to get over. Botham listened and appeared to take note, but less than two weeks later I watched him throw away his wicket on the second day of the Old Trafford Test against the leg-spin of Trevor Hohns. With England in trouble, Botham had received only six balls when he charged down the pitch, slogged, missed and was bowled for nought. Probably he had thrashed Hohns a bit in the nets when they were team-mates at Queensland and thought he could throw the bat again, but really it was an incredibly careless shot for a man aiming to prove a point. At his best, he has got away with chancing his arm, but those days are behind him.

The major back operation that Botham underwent in the summer of 1988 really marked the beginning of the end. It clearly finished him as a great bowler because after it he could no longer put a lot of body into his action to gain pace. He was unable to pivot and turn to bowl his famous fast outswingers. The supple body and slim waist of his younger days disappeared under the extra weight he put on over the years. His great asset as a bowler was his hostility, and I rate him second only to Fred Trueman as a man who could rip through the tail. There is nothing so frustrating for an opening batsman as a stubborn rearguard action by the bottom half of the opposition order. Once I had got it into my mind that I would be batting soon, I hated to hang about and in Test matches I always pressed the captain to use Botham. 'Get the gorilla on quick,' I used to shout to Brearley. There was no messing about with Botham, who did not worry too much about dropping it short. He could bat well enough to defend himself, so the possibility of retaliation did not concern him, and his success rate in this direction will stand comparison with anyone's. Once he lost that keen, cutting edge of pace, however, his bowling became ordinary.

We met at the NatWest Cup Final in September 1988. 'I'll get my share of wickets in the championship,' he told me, and I warned him of the difficulties that lay ahead. He was recovering from surgery. 'No doubt you will,' I replied. 'A lot of county batsmen will be a bit apprehensive when you bowl, but not many Test batsmen will worry, because all you've got is gentle swing now.' Botham has enjoyed a lot of latitude from the public and the authorities down the years because of his great performances on the field, but as he finds it increasingly difficult to deliver the goods I am convinced that people will turn against him. It is so easy to become the poor man's Muhammad Ali – a braggart with no talent and a figure of fun living on hopes and fantasy.

Botham's excesses have encouraged the yob culture in cricket, epitomized by the noisy, usually drunk, gangs of youths who have spoiled many a Saturday or Sunday afternoon for the decent, informed cricket-watcher. His belligerent approach somehow conveyed to these hooligans the thought that it was all right to break the rules and lash out. They reacted to each other in the way he reacted out in the middle, so they became dangerous as they splashed their drink about and pushed and fought. He did not encourage their presence knowingly, but he gave substance to their cause, and the occasional rumours of his macho excesses provided for their bad behaviour a thin cloak of respectability in their own minds. They will not readily forgive him when he lets them down, for there is no-one easier to ridicule and despise than yesterday's hero when he is still clinging grimly to centre-stage.

The tragedy for Botham is that in his mind he keeps remembering the good old days and he thinks they will come back. An integral part of his make-up was the belief that he could achieve anything he set his heart on. For a while greatness has been only just out of reach, which means he finds it hard to accept that he cannot hope to touch it again. The danger is that he will keep on for too long and become a sad figure. To some extent Ted Dexter, as England supremo, encouraged him to contemplate the impossible by telling the media that the Test team needed him for the 1990 West Indies tour. Manager Micky Stewart talked to Botham about making himself available during the Nottingham Test against Australia, a decision which soon became public property. I could not see any logic in Dexter's thinking and I told Botham at Scarborough that he would not be spending the winter in the Caribbean. 'Oh, I'll go all right,' he insisted. 'I've never made a century against the West Indies and I'd like another crack at them. I'll soon be back bowling from my full run at pace as well.' He kidded no-one except himself. At least I was honest and while he may not have liked what I had to say, it represented the truth. England kidded him along and then publicly humiliated him, which was shabby treatment for a man they have relied on so often.

Arguably, Botham messed up his big chance to revive his career when he fell out of favour with Queensland in March 1988. He had put himself on course to become a cricket millionaire when he signed a contract with the Australian state with deals such as £40,000 from a food chain; £30,000 from Ansett, the Australian airline; £20,000 from a car manufacturer and a wine firm; and £30,000 from a major brewery. When he arrived in Brisbane to begin a scheduled three-year association with Queensland he had an excellent opportunity to start a new life with a new team and a new public.

He proudly proclaimed: 'I still believe I'm the best and I aim to prove it.' His debut for Queensland at the Gabba attracted the biggest attendance since the days of Don Bradman, and he gave value for money with 58 from thirty-four balls. Fred Bennett, chairman of the New South Wales Cricket Association, admitted: 'We've got to hand it to Ian. He's probably the biggest draw card in cricket.' Things continued to run smoothly as Queensland made good progress towards their first Sheffield Shield triumph in fifty-six years, but trouble lay just around the corner. Botham and Dennis Lillee were involved in a disturbance during which six hundred pounds' worth of damage was done to a club-house. Then an umpire reported Botham for 'using obscene language' in the game against Victoria and he received a £200 fine. Worse followed. Botham missed official practice to play in a special match organized by Ansett and then flew on to Perth for the Sheffield Shield final between Queensland and Western Australia. A mid-air row resulted in Botham grabbing a passenger's head and shaking it, a stupid action which he tried to justify by saying: 'If he'd kept his nose out of an argument that had nothing to do with him, none of the trouble would have happened.' More fines were levied – £350 by the court that heard the case of his mid-air assault and £2,000 by the Australian Cricket Board, but the biggest blow came when Queensland sacked him. Greg Chappell, the former Queensland and Australian captain, bitterly disappointed by their defeat in the Shield final commented: 'We'll never win anything until we get some discipline in the team.'

That marked the end of a brief if stormy chapter in Botham's career. Although he has played on with Worcestershire, Ian Botham, great allrounder and flawed genius, is on the way down.

7

Boy wonder

David Gower has been the 'boy wonder' of English cricket almost from the time he made his début for Leicestershire in 1975, but fifteen years later, at the start of the 1990 season, his career was clearly at an important crossroads. Left out of the 1990 England tour to the West Indies after being captain against Australia the previous summer, he moved to Hampshire in search of inspiration.

The stylish left-hander has suffered over a long period from having too much talent, for everything comes easily to him. From the start his elegance and effortless stroke-play marked him out as much better than average and he enjoyed the benefits of a public school education. He was, in fact, a natural for the England captaincy, yet he made a horrible mess of the job. Even when he luckily got a second chance he could not concentrate his mind sufficiently to make a go of it.

There is no doubt that his omission from the England touring party to the Caribbean represented a major setback for a player used to success and adulation. I might well have taken him, although I have no strong opinion, and I think that the selectors left him out to shake him up, to make him realize that no-one has a divine right to be chosen for England. Micky Stewart does not like Gower's flippant attitude and he decided after the débâcle against Australia, when his job as England manager was very much on the line, that he had to assert his authority. He appreciated the need to bring about a much tougher, more professional approach, and he could not be sure that Gower would knuckle down. Stewart had to take account of the danger that Gower would decide to go his own way, setting the younger players a bad example. Gower spent most of the 1989 summer troubled by a painful shoulder, which required surgery, although he maintained that he would be fit for the West Indies. I did not believe that, nor did Stewart, who felt that Gower's batting had become restricted.

On balance, therefore, Stewart decided not to take a gamble on Gower's fitness or his approach. Graham Gooch was also worried about Gower, and he had the sense to be pragmatic even though they are good friends. He could not afford to be sentimental, and he put the squad first. Gooch no doubt also took into consideration the fact that Gower had had only a moderately successful series against the West Indies the last time round, in 1988. Gooch took over the captaincy for the final Test of that summer at the Oval, where Gower was dropped. Gower went to see the team play anyway, and spoke to Gooch, emphasizing how keen he was to go on tour to India that winter. He stressed that he thought he was running into some better form. Gooch was not convinced, however. He told me he would obviously like a fit and enthusiastic Gower in his squad, but that he could not be sure of his commitment. The question in Gooch's mind concerned how hungry Gower was to play and whether he would be ready to get his head down and fight. It was one thing for Gower to say he was very keen and another altogether to prove it with deeds. Gooch discussed the whole business with me and when Gower finally got a place on the tour it was a marginal decision.

I argued that Gower ought to go because having a good left-hander could be useful if the pitches offered some turn, and this point may just have swayed the balance.

The switch from Leicestershire cannot have been an easy decision because they have been very good to Gower. They made him captain even when he could not be regularly available, they gave him an excellent benefit and, most important, they backed him loyally. Gower may never realize just how much he owes to the club. At the same time, a fresh start in new pastures may prove to be the long-term stimulus that Gower needs. He faces a new county public and presumably wants to impress, but he has to display a greater degree of consistency by carrying his form through from the early months. There is a big difference between being keen in April and May and retaining that desire to do well throughout the summer and into September. The cricket season is a long, gruelling haul. Gower can no longer live on the memory of the runs he has accumulated in the past.

I believe England should make him earn any further Test honours the hard way, by scoring runs regularly in the county championship. Gower has not, as a matter of record, done much in the domestic competitions for quite a while. In 1988, for example, he waited until August for his first century, while the following summer brought an early double-century and nothing else. I suspect that in the future he is going to have to demand selection for England, to force them to pick him by figuring prominently in the Hampshire team. A run of good scores would inevitably push him into the headlines. Newspapers never shy away from telling the selectors what they should or should not do and at some stage there is certain to be a campaign on his behalf, just as there was when England endured some shaky moments in the later stages of the West Indies tour.

I have come to the conclusion that if Gower does have anything more to offer Test cricket he has got to move higher up the order. He should not be allowed to hide away at number four or five, even though he likes it down there. His admirers contend that he is better in the middle order, but we would all find it easier away from the new ball and the pace bowlers when they are fresh and bowling flat out. England is beginning to make some strides forward with a group of promising young batsmen, including Alec Stewart, Rob Bailey, Robin Smith, Nasser Hussain, Michael Atherton and Richard Blakey. They all lack experience and should not be thrown in at the deep end ahead of Gower. If he does genuinely want to play for England and do his bit for the country, he should be ready to go in much earlier. At thirty-two, with over a hundred Tests to his credit, he ought to be happy to shoulder the responsibility for shaping and holding together an innings. England cannot go on protecting him. I have told Gooch that Gower should be up there at number three, or even opening. If I had suddenly decided that I wanted an easier life at four or five, there would have been hell in the England dressing-room and in the press. Actually what Gower could do for the up-and-coming batsmen is a lot more important than anything he could do for himself.

Gower should also take a long, hard look at the way in which he has been getting out down the years. It is all very well for a novice to play some flashy shots outside the off stump and get out occasionally as a result. People make allowances for the impetuosity of youth, but they also expect the older and better players to learn from their mistakes, and this Gower has failed to do. He was playing much the same way in 1989 as he had done in 1975, which is stupid. A lot of experienced cricket-watchers have become disenchanted with Gower, which is why this move to Hampshire represents a last chance. If he is not careful he will toss away the respect he has earned by dint of his more successful innings down the years.

He must be aware that his recent home Test record is more than a little disappointing. Look at his scores for England in the three years 1987–9: 22, 8, 10, 55, 61, 18,

28, 34, 18, 88, 46, 1, 9, 34, 13, 2, 26, 34, 57, 106, 8, 35, 15, 11, 5, 79 and 7. He is better than that, but he needs to take a long look in the mirror. It is possible to fool other people, to make excuses or gloss over the realities, but nobody can fool the man in the mirror. The problem for him is that, like the rest of us, he will discover that his physical powers decline slowly and steadily with age. Ability starts to wane in the mid-thirties. It becomes that little bit more difficult to get in the right positions. The great players have had to compensate by working at their technique and fitness and by using their heads to take advantage of their experience.

I know from experience how important it is to play the percentage shots, but Gower has tended to rely on his instincts and they are likely to become less reliable. It is not too late for him at the moment, but it soon will be if he is not careful and thoughtful. Unfortunately, he is not serious for very long and always there is the flip side of his character lurking just below the surface. This was very evident on the 1979–80 tour to Australia. Some general rules are always applied to routine business, like team meetings, and everyone is expected to be punctual. As an extra incentive we levied fines at one pound per minute for anyone who turned up late and in Sydney Gower became a victim of the system. When he did arrive he was casual as ever and attempted to make a joke of his apology. Mike Brearley cut him down to size very simply and quickly in front of everyone. If Gower had just come into the room, said he was sorry and sat down nothing more would have been said. With the best of intentions, anyone can be late, but Gower could not resist trying to be funny and it did not go down too well with the captain when the rest of us had been kept waiting.

I would not advise him to change his game, for his natural talent is something to be treasured, but I advise him to round off some of the sloppy edges. It would pay him to think a bit more about what he is trying to do and what he wants out of life. Definitely I expect him to drift out of the game very quickly if he doesn't command a fairly regular Test place over the next couple of years. He likes the glamour and is not too taken with the long slog of the county circuit, which is probably why he does not have much of a cricket brain. He is intelligent and has been quite academic in his time, but that is not the same thing as really understanding cricket. To do that, you have to take a keen interest in all that goes on.

I enjoyed batting with him very much. He is a very pleasant lad and we have never had a cross word because there is nothing to dislike about him. But he is not like me in any way. Cricket has meant everything to me, to him it is nothing more than a good life, providing him with the opportunity to put his name in lights and bask in the adulation of the spectators and commentators. He can take cricket or leave it. Gower understates everything so as not to show any feelings, and I was not surprised to learn that his father had been involved in the diplomatic service.

I cannot pretend to know what, if anything, motivates him because it is impossible to get inside his mind. Only occasionally have I seen any substance in him; most times everything is just skin deep. I don't recall his ever showing any real emotion, even when he completed a century or played particularly well. He is a master in the art of non-communication, relying on the quick quip, although Tony Lewis believes he might be confused and inwardly shattered by the criticism that surrounded his 1989 captaincy. Tony took part in a cricket forum with Gower at the Barbican Centre in London in December 1989. Brian Johnston chaired the evening, which involved questions and answers, together with some films, and attracted an audience of almost three thousand people. Gower, as ever, was very laid back and casual until a member of the audience pinned him down with some very shrewd questions. Lewis was surprised to hear Gower produce an excellent series of answers expressing good, reasoned views, something he never did to his players as captain.

Perhaps Gower suffered from being made captain, for he rarely showed any aptitude for the job and I suspect that man-to-man relationships worried him. He was simply dreadful in the West Indies in 1986, when I went out to do some writing for *The Mail on Sunday*. Players were almost encouraged to turn up to practise in a wide and unsuitable variety of shirts, shorts and footwear, while, with nets optional, some of the party took the opportunity to have a free holiday, spending their time sailing, swimming or on the beach. The whole tour degenerated into a farce. Barbados is traditionally the island that most English supporters visit to cheer on the team and have a break, and the weather that year was perfect except for some heavy overnight showers. These made the practice pitches too wet to be used in the morning, so Gower gave his squad the day off after a few exercises and a bit of catching practice. It never entered his head to call them back at 3.00p.m. or 4.00p.m., by which time the nets had dried out.

I imagine that Gower and the rest of the players enjoyed another day off in paradise, but they paid a heavy price when England crashed to defeat in three and a half days before thousands of their supporters, who had spent a lot of money to fly out and encourage them. Many spectators were very upset at the quality of the English cricket and were left wondering whether Gower was in charge of a cricket team or a motley crew of holiday-makers. I wanted to prepare for what turned out to be my last season with Yorkshire, so Desmond Haynes and I found a ground just a few miles down the road from the Kensington Oval and paid a local groundsman to prepare a batting strip. The area was more like a wasteland with a square big enough for perhaps six or eight pitches in a season, but the chap did a good job and we went back every afternoon before the Test, including the rest day, to bat against Franklyn Stephenson, Hartley Alleyne and Ricky Ellcock. I got in a lot of excellent practice and had gone some way towards getting my eye in when I reported to Headingley in April, so it was possible to get nets if you cared enough. England presumably did not take enough trouble to look around, for Barbados is a tiny island, little more than eleven miles by nine miles. It was ridiculous really. I got better practice than the England players and my season was still a month away, while they were bracing themselves for an immediate ordeal by pace.

You simply could not make any excuses for the manner in which Gower led England on that tour. On that basis, Gower should have ruled himself out of further consideration for the captaincy, but Dexter made a big thing of bringing him back against the 1989 Australians. For his part, Gower, ignoring the lessons of the past, made it plain that he intended to do things his way, pushing Stewart into a back seat. Stewart, working with Dexter in a new partnership, was in a difficult situation, a bit unsure of how far his authority stretched and how much he could say.

The Test and County Cricket Board had put Dexter in charge overall, so he had the final say, and, to make matters worse, Stewart and Gower were never on the same wavelength. Stewart earned everything that came his way through sheer hard work, backed up by careful thought and preparation. He is nobody's fool and has been around for a long time, being both captain and then manager at Surrey. Although he gained only limited experience at the top level, with eight Tests and one tour to India in 1963, Stewart can handle people and he understands what makes them tick. To stand by and watch Gower squander a second golden opportunity with his lacklustre, flippant approach must have been so frustrating for him.

Cricket captains are judged on the results of the teams they lead and on the general level of performance. England under Gower reflected his easy-going nature, having occasional highs and depressing lows. Having come into office on a temporary basis when Bob Willis was injured in Pakistan in 1982 and 1983–4, Gower won a series 2–1 in India in 1984–5 and supervised an Ashes triumph over the 1985 Australians, but he also lost ten consecutive

Tests to the West Indies. Gower is not a motivator in the Brearley mould, nor a shrewd manipulator of situations like Illingworth. I cannot believe he does much homework on the opposition, which is probably why he allowed Allan Border to dictate the 1989 series over here. The casual observer would never have guessed who was in charge on the field; far too often for comfort bowlers operated at the wrong end to the wrong field. It appeared to be a case of posting two slips and telling everyone else to spread out.

So many times Gower appeared to let games drift along, with his side being carried away by the course of events. Some backsides needed kicking, but Gower was never the man to exert his authority. Watching the Barbados Test in 1986 I would see four or five men out in the middle all waving their arms about when the field was being set, something that never happened when either Brearley or Illingworth was in charge.

At times Gower infuriates me and I would like to get hold of him and shake him just to see if there is any reaction. I care so much about cricket in general and my batting in particular that it can affect me emotionally. Gower keeps a tight rein on his feelings, showing neither elation nor disappointment. In the Perth Test of the 1978–9 tour, when I performed well below my normal standards because I could not clear my mind of the troubles with Yorkshire, I told him: 'I wish I could bat like you.' He made batting look so simple then and I paid him an honest compliment, which took him by surprise.

On the other side of the coin, however, during that Test I noticed a real chink in his armour, which is still there. Rodney Hogg went round the wicket to him for a couple of overs, firing the ball in at his body, tucking him up for room and making him look distinctly poor. Hogg didn't get him out, though, and went back over the wicket. Similarly, in the West Indies tour of 1986 Gower struggled in the same area. Courtney Walsh bowled at his ribs in the game against Jamaica, causing him acute embarrassment, so the whole of the West Indies pace attack took the same line in the Kingston Test and Gower never looked like making a run. Now that tells me something about his attitude. He must have realized that he had a weak spot in 1979, but seven years later he had done nothing about it, leaving himself vulnerable at the highest level. Even in 1989 the Australians succeeded against him by setting traps around the leg stump. This resistance to change makes me wonder if he can adapt his game.

His own comments on the dreadful series against the Australians are also very revealing. He blundered badly in surrendering the initiative from day one by putting in the tourists when he won the toss at Headingley. He admitted afterwards: 'When the brains trust convened at Headingley we talked about cloud cover rather than other things and I bowed to the view that we should leave out the spinner and field first. I have regretted that ever since.' That smacks to me of passing the buck. Gower had made it clear, as I have said, that he took the captaincy almost on his own terms, so he was in a position to ignore all advice. In fact, he chose to listen to the 'brains trust' instead of to groundsman Keith Boyce, who told him to bat first if he got the chance. 'Losing was just a blip,' he said, brushing aside criticism, and went on to create the impression that he could see nothing wrong in all that he had done. At Lord's, with his side deeper in trouble, he conceded: 'We have had a couple of hiccups.'

It is this kind of arrogance which made so many people angry and left the England side in confusion. In that sense the summer of 1989 summed up his career to date – so much talent, so many disappointments – could have done better.

8

Black and white

The unofficial tour to South Africa by Mike Gatting and a group of prominent English cricketers managed by Gloucestershire's David Graveney did not come as any surprise to me. The only people who had not seen it coming were the members of the Test and County Cricket Board, who buried their heads in the sand like ostriches and pretended it would never happen. The hysterical reaction in certain quarters was equally predictable, as the whole question of cricket and South Africa is persistently distorted by hypocrisy. The players who took the big decision to sacrifice their official Test careers were accused of being selfish by, amongst others, athletes anxious to protect the Commonwealth Games being held in New Zealand at much the same time. Sprint star John Regis leapt on to the bandwagon to launch a vicious personal attack on two black cricketers, Middlesex's Roland Butcher and Lancashire's Phil DeFreitas, who had agreed to join Gatting's squad, but then changed their minds when their families were threatened with violence. 'They have betrayed all black sportsmen and black people,' he claimed, adding: 'It has sickened me so much that if they came up to me and tried to explain to my face why they did it I would just turn and walk away from them. It could have serious repercussions for so many other sportsmen and women. These guys could ruin things for athletes, boxers and swimmers who have worked so hard for the Commonwealth Games.' Middle-distance ace Steve Cram rushed to join in, but it seemed to me that their real concern was for their own sport. So long as the Games went ahead, they didn't seem to care about anything else.

Butcher and DeFreitas found themselves under a lot of pressure, publicly and privately, from athletes with big mouths. Butcher in particular needed the substantial money available from South Africa and I did not notice athletes showing any interest in helping him out, although Cram, for example, can get between £10,000 and £20,000 per race; compare that with the £15,000 that a county cricketer can expect from a full season.

The high moral tone adopted by athletes, including the politically ambitious Sebastian Coe interested me because I cannot recall any of them refusing to compete against Russia or any of the Eastern Bloc countries. The denial of human rights by the Communist countries was presumably all right so far as they were concerned, and they didn't seem to me to make too much fuss when South African-born Zola Budd suddenly and miraculously became a British runner. Their arguments sounded reasonable only to those who did not look below the surface.

Coe entered the arena on the day Gatting and his party went to South Africa. He was speaking from New Zealand, where, as his athletics career drew to a close, he was preparing to become a politician. He made what he no doubt felt were a number of telling points; arguing that Gatting and his squad let down the whole country, that he, Coe, was speaking out for the majority of English people, and that he would never visit South Africa in any capacity, not even as a politician. His points could be easily answered, however. Yes, of course all professional sportsmen have to sell their skills in the market-place. That is how they earn their living.

Coe took part in the Moscow Olympics, where he had a chance of medals and glory, despite that country's invasion of Afghanistan. No doubt he will be a success if he gets elected to Westminster – although I would not trust him. Coe claims to speak as the voice of the British people. He is a long way from becoming Prime Minister, and was not even a member of Parliament when he took it upon himself to represent the country.

Many people with whom I come into contact are sick of people like Coe, Cram and Regis telling them what to do and what to think. A lot of ordinary citizens are afraid to speak their own minds, because anyone who sees any good at all in South Africa is labelled racist. When opposition to the Gatting tour took the form of picketing, at grounds all over the country, cricket followers demonstrated their feelings clearly enough by sending the political agitators packing.

More and more people in all walks of life are becoming aware that their freedom is being eroded. Any individual should be able to visit South Africa for any purpose. That is a democratic right that no-one should be able to take away.

Obviously Coe and those who think like him have the right to put their case strongly and try to persuade others by sensible argument, but if we in Britain reach the stage at which there is only one way to do anything or approach any situation, then we will have become Marxist. The trouble is that the views of the silent majority, the millions who just want to behave decently and get on with their own lives, are seldom heard. The headline-seekers are forever on the air or in newspapers hammering away with their propaganda. I don't know how Coe can be such an assured expert on conditions in South Africa if he does not monitor the changes. As Yorkshire's Paul Jarvis observed when he returned home from the Gatting trip: 'There are a lot of people talking about South Africa who have never bothered to find out for themselves what the situation is.' I have been to South Africa many times since 1964 and, while I hold no brief for apartheid, which is a sickening system destined for the scrap-heap, I do like to see fair play. The whole situation cries out for more balanced judgements. Take Australian Prime Minister Bob Hawke, for example. He is a fierce and emotional critic of apartheid, ever ready to lash out at South Africa, and often Britain as well, whenever he sees the chance of shouting into a microphone. However, I've never heard him say anything about the plight of the aborigines in the business and sporting life of his own country and how badly the whites have treated them – yet it does not seem to be internationally fashionable to raise that issue.

Another fact persistently overlooked is that black Africans have a much better life in South Africa than in most other parts of the continent. There is reasonably sound evidence to indicate that some 50,000 Somalis were judicially murdered in 1989, that thousands of Ethiopians were driven at gunpoint from their villages by their government around the same time, that Mauritania allows slavery among its people – yet all the time South Africa is harangued in the dock of world opinion. No nation in modern times has earned such notoriety in terms of supposed human wickedness.

I am well aware that respected figures such as Archbishop Desmond Tutu argue that sporting links with South Africa should be broken until such time as apartheid is ended, and I respect their right to pursue a cause they obviously think is just. However, there are one or two obvious questions. Where were Archbishop Tutu and his fellow-thinkers when England, New Zealand and Australia toured South Africa before 1970? Cricket was one hundred per cent the white man's province then. Hardly any coloureds watched or played and the comparatively tiny areas into which the black spectators were admitted were surrounded by fences ten to twelve feet in height. Why did the agitators not speak out then? Why didn't they demonstrate? The plight of the coloured races was much worse then and I speak from experience, having seen for myself the improvements. The fact is that cricket now is totally integrated from both the playing and watching point of view, yet it is being made a sacrificial pawn on a vast political chess-board. Why should sport shoulder the burden of protest? Everybody is aware that businessmen trade with South Africa.

Just for the record, an article in the *Sunday Express* in late 1989 stated that ninety-nine major British companies still held half the equity of South African companies. A further twenty-one held a further ten per cent. Among them were some of the biggest names in the country, including BAT Industries, Beecham Group, Blue Circle, British Oxygen, British Petroleum, Cadbury Schweppes (one-time sponsors of county cricket), Coats Viyella, Courtaulds, Fisons, General Accident, General Electric, Glaxo, Hansons, ICI, Lucas Industries, Marley, Portals Group, Racal Chubb, Rowntree, Shell, Thorn EMI, Tootal and Wimpey. Britain's exports to South Africa totalled £1,075 million and imports £800 million in 1988. The British Overseas Trade Board, part of the Department of Trade and Industry, even produces two publications – *Hints to Exporters, Southern Africa,* and *Country Profile, South Africa* – to help stimulate commercial relationships. Nor does the double-dealing stop there. Black African nations also trade with South Africa, carefully removing the labels from tins before passing them down the commercial line.

Just as the South African government discriminates on the basis of colour, our politicians discriminate on the basis of convenience. Cricket is an easy target. The argument in favour of a sporting boycott rests on the theory that without foreign competition cricket and other sports in South Africa will die, with the result that the government will be forced to dismantle apartheid more quickly. That may just be true, but the Afrikaner instinctively shies away from the thought of surrender. The more he is threatened

Torrid times in the West Indies; Robin Smith batting in the fifth Test, Antigua 1990.

England's main strike bowlers on the 1990 West Indies tour: Devon Malcolm, **(above)**; Gladstone Small **(right)**; and Angus Fraser, **(opposite)**.

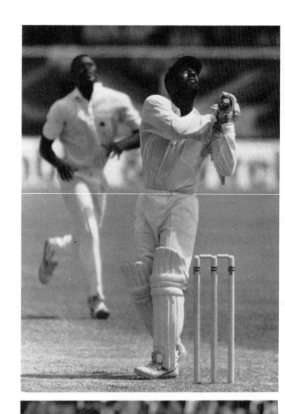

'Masterblaster' Vivian
Richards is able to get away
with outrageous strokes.
Here **(top)** he hits out
against Devon Malcolm in
the fourth Test in Barbados,
during an extraordinary over
in which he scored 18.
But he didn't always get
away with it in the 1990
series: for example, when
he was bowled by Malcolm
in the first Test at Sabina
Park, Jamaica **(bottom)**.

Richards runs up the pitch waving his arms and Bailey is given out, fourth Test in Barbados, 1990. Such appealing puts the umpires under intolerable pressure and needs to be stopped by the authorities.

David Gower leaves
the wicket having
scored 7 in the sixth
Test against Australia
at The Oval in 1989
(top), probably his last
ever as England
captain. Left out of
the England side for
the 1990 tour of the
West Indies, he found
a new role writing for
The Times **(bottom)**.

Sadly, Ian Botham's great days are over. He is no longer able to bowl with the same pace or movement which made him the leading wicket-taker in Test history (until overtaken by Richard Hadlee), and he has not yet found the application to earn him a Test place for his batting alone. These pictures show him playing in the fourth Test against Australia at Old Trafford in 1989.

Practice, practice practice...

the more he withdraws into the laager mentality and, as in the old pioneering days, he pulls the horses and wagons into a circle to defend himself.

Indeed, the organization of Gatting's pirate tour stemmed directly from the refusal of the 1989 International Cricket Conference to give the South African delegation even a glimmer of hope for the future. Raman Subba Row, the chairman of the Test and County Cricket Board, declined to talk to them, officially or unofficially. He did not consult either the counties or his executive, but closed the door on any hope of contact. He did so despite overwhelming evidence that South African cricket is now truly multi-racial and that the game's officials have been leading figures in breaking down racial barriers. The fact is that cricket is a growing passion among black youngsters. The South African Cricket Union took the game to the townships and sparked an explosion of interest, which was inevitable as the kids have little else to do. Cricket offered them an alternative to roaming the streets getting into trouble and black youngsters quickly made great strides forward.

This process began after the Basil D'Oliveira incident, which prevented England from touring South Africa in 1968–9. It certainly focused attention on the situation and made people more aware of what was going on, although the events leading up to his eventual selection had caused a few eyebrows to be raised. I hurt my back in the third Test of 1968 at Edgbaston and did not play in the fourth and fifth Tests against Australia. After being out of action for two months, I took part in the Scarborough Festival to test my fitness, and then joined the International Cavaliers for a brief tour of Cornwall and Devon. Fred Trueman, Gary Sobers, Rohan Kanhai and Lance Gibbs were among the Cavaliers and they were all stunned when D'Oliveira was not selected for the original party to South Africa. The whole business amounted to a farce, for he had played in the final Test at the Oval and made a century. The selectors – Alec Bedser, Don Kenyon, Peter May, and chairman Doug

Insole – had met on 27 August, and they were joined by captain Colin Cowdrey, manager Les Ames, Arthur Gilligan and Gubby Allen, respectively president and treasurer of the MCC. The meeting had lasted some six hours and when it was learned that D'Oliveira had been omitted there was an uproar from former England cricketer the Reverend David Sheppard, MPs and others. However, D'Oliveira was called into the ranks on 16 September, when one of the original selections, Warwickshire seamer Tom Cartwright, reported unfit. The result, of course, was that the tour did not go ahead. When the decision not to go had been taken, the MCC made a very important statement: 'The committee were informed that the side selected to represent MCC in South Africa is not acceptable for reasons beyond the control of the South African Cricket Union.' In other words, the South African government had played the decisive role in banning D'Oliveira; no doubt they had worked on the basis that a decision to use him, a batsman, as a replacement for Cartwright, a bowler, did not make any cricket sense.

The Cricket Union realized that it had to take independent action. Going it alone, it brought about a miracle in the shape of integrated cricket watched by integrated crowds in a segregated country. They believed the Test and County Cricket Board who promised to do their best to get them re-admitted to the International Cricket Conference if they did not sponsor rebel tours. The South African Cricket Union remained utterly independent and refused government funding as they went their own way in tearing down the racial barriers. They met the requirements of the International Cricket Conference only to find that no-one was prepared to acknowledge what they had done. They deserved much better treatment following all their hard work. Perhaps it is significant that many of the leading cricket officials in South Africa, including the president Joe Pamensky and the managing director Ali Bacher are Jewish, and thus very sensitive to issues of race, colour and creed. It is worth noting, too, that in 1989 Subba Row, as chairman of the Test and County Cricket Board, accepted the restrictions on freedom of movement imposed by the International Cricket Conference. If any individual goes to South Africa now, he is banned from playing Test cricket for four years. Subba Row fancies himself as a mediator, a peacemaker with a glib tongue; he is happy to achieve a settlement at any price, but he leaves cricket to pick up the bill.

Finding the door slammed in their face, the South Africans felt they had to defend their position. Bacher, a former Test captain, told me: 'We don't want to be defiant. We want to be part of world cricket. We want to bring about changes in apartheid through cricket. But when the International Cricket Conference wouldn't listen, even unofficially, we had to look after our own interests.' South Africans wanted to play and watch cricket at the highest level, and England had a reservoir of disillusioned talent. The Test and County Cricket Board might well have huffed and puffed about loyalty, but loyalty is a two-way thing. Was the Test and County Cricket Board loyal to Gatting over the England captaincy? Was it loyal to Chris Cowdrey, who was promised the captaincy against the West Indies for two Tests in 1988 and then sacked after missing the second through injury?

Most of the players who went with Gatting were worried about their financial security and felt that they could not rely on the game continuing to provide them with a good living. Neil Foster, from Essex, had knee and back injuries to concern him, while Worcestershire's Graham Dilley was also troubled with a dodgy knee. Even Jarvis, who, on paper at least, had a genuine Test future, nursed doubts about his back standing up to the endless strain of quick bowling. Who had the right to say to these young men with wives and families that they should sacrifice the £120,000 they would have earned for two tours? They would have had to play in just about every Test for five years to earn that sort of money with England.

Had Foster continued to make himself available to England and then broken down, he would no doubt have received a lot of sympathy, but that hardly pays the bills. What good is talent to a sportsman if he does not use it to secure his future? Plenty of famous sporting personalities have finished on the breadline after giving their public many memorable moments to savour. There are a lot of ifs and buts in Test cricket, and many good players have retired wondering just why they did not get picked on a permanent basis. Any player with fitness worries must therefore regard the chance to guarantee himself a sizeable sum with some enthusiasm. Graham Dilley, for example, had the opportunity to go with the 1982 unofficial party to South Africa and was certainly tempted then, but he finally declined. He does not like regular touring and being away from home, but in 1989 he was offered a second opportunity. Eight years further down the hard road of first-class cricket, the chance to earn a 'pot of gold' proved too much to resist.

It was suggested in some ill-informed quarters that Gatting's tourists had left English cricket in a mess, but, as Peter Roebuck, the one-time Somerset captain, explained: 'English cricket was already in a mess. The rebellion was symptomatic of the disease, not its cause.'

Roebuck was right. Those players who chose to go to South Africa were by no means the only ones disenchanted with English cricket. The leadership has commanded little or no respect for many years. Money was one factor in the complicated equation, discontent another. Cricketers have lost faith in the selection process and resent the way in which they are used and discarded. There is little pride left in representing England, and Lord's officials should have realized long ago that there was something fundamentally wrong with the way they have been running the game.

Very few people realize how many big-name cricketers have discussed the possibility of playing in South Africa.

In fact the prospects of an official West Indian tour of South Africa are fascinating. If the slow move towards democracy gathers any sort of momentum the visit of the best black cricketers in the world could spark a tremendous explosion of interest among the black population. Such a move might unearth a lot of talent and open many doors for youngsters with limited opportunities in other directions. Those who constantly seek to destroy contacts with South Africa might profitably consider that scenario.

Gatting's tour, however, did more harm than good because nothing had been thought through properly. One of the immediate casualties was the township cricket, which, as we have seen, was an important part of the South African Cricket Union's programme to broaden multi-racial participation. For example, the 3M Rocklands Cricket Club near Bloemfontein suspended all cricket under the auspices of the Orange Free State Cricket Union in February 1990. 'The step became necessary because of the threats of violence,' a spokesman explained. 'It is so sad that youngsters from the townships have been denied the right to play the sport they love.' The club ran thirteen teams in various senior and school leagues and officials worked hard to resume normal activities as soon as possible, but the whole business was a serious blow to cricket officials.

The trip was also mishandled from the start, as soon as the names were announced in early August. This may have appeared to be an honourable thing to do, putting everything on an open and honest footing, although the suspicion grew that the South Africans were really throwing down the gauntlet. In any case, circumstances contrived to give the media and the anti-apartheid organizations the chance to pillory the players. Small bands of noisy agitators gathered at many county grounds; Butcher and DeFreitas, in particular, became targets for the rabble-rousers. The news should not have been released until shortly before the tour was due to take place, allowing the players to escape such pressures. The long time-gap between one event and the other meant that emotions ran high. The tour should have taken place in November, when the South African Cricket Union would have received more publicity. By staging it after Christmas the organizers found themselves competing for space in the media with the official England tour to the West Indies, with the Five Nations' Rugby Union Championship, and with the exciting developments in the Football League and the FA Cup.

Gatting was stuck in a no-win situation as he marched out bravely to talk to the protesters. Politics was always going to be of greater news value than cricket, whatever line he took. And Gatting's team never had much of a chance on the field, for they had not been in action for four months and lacked match practice. So whichever way you look at things, the timing was all wrong.

The shambolic nature of the Gatting tour proved conclusively that we were right to keep our plans secret and present a stunned cricket world with a *fait accompli* in 1982. At the time we were accused of using secrecy to hide our shame and the media could neither understand nor accept our silence. As ever, they worked on the misguided theory that they had a right to make us explain our actions. Some media men tried to make us defend ourselves, as though we had committed some sort of crime.

I never doubted the wisdom of confidentiality. Why give hysterical, emotional idealists the chance to interfere with your plans? Gatting and some other members of his party have tried to put forward their points of view and the captain attempted to talk sensibly to demonstrators both at home and in South Africa, but he was wasting his time. The whole protest movement is orchestrated by hardliners, who are strong on individual freedom until it cuts across their activities. Then it's a case of 'do what we want or we will make life very unpleasant for you'. The simple answer is the one we gave in 1982. We said firmly at every turn that we were professionals earning our living with the talent we possessed. My one regret from that occasion was that the whole England team did not go to play one Test in April after the tour to India, as had been planned. Botham, Gower and Willis were all more than a little interested in that idea, and there would not have been much the Test and County Cricket Board could have done. I doubt whether they could have suspended all the senior players.

The future remains confused, despite the cancellation of a second visit by Gatting, originally scheduled for 1991. For a start, the political situation is so terribly complicated. The Dutch and others of European stock built up the country, fighting some famous and bloody battles, notably against the Zulus, in the process, and they achieved a degree of prosperity they are reluctant to give away. They do not want to see their standards and influence decline, and they are passionately opposed to one-man, one-vote. They feel that they would be overwhelmed, as has happened in Zimbabwe, Tanzania and Uganda. This, as I see it, is the heart of the matter. I know there are many white people in South Africa who accept that apartheid will have to be dismantled in the comparatively near future. They merely worry about the consequences.

It is easy for those not directly concerned to have simplistic views. I feel sure that many of the people offering cheap advice would think differently if they were being asked to sacrifice all that they and their ancestors had worked hard for down the years. One-man, one-vote would not bring power-sharing to South Africa because such a system would guarantee a total dominance by black voters. I have no doubt the advantages held by the minority, who control the majority, should be removed, but some recognition has to be given to the contribution made by whites in the past. There is too much outside interference in the affairs of South Africa, which is hindering rather than helping social development. I remain convinced that most progress will be made if steps are taken gradually but not too slowly, with education being given priority. In this area, cricket has already shown the way, responding to promises made by the International Cricket Conference, only to be let down.

The South African Cricket Union has now entered into talks with the sporting arm of the African National Congress, although whether they will be accepted back into official world cricket remains to be seen. The South Africans do not appear to have grasped the fact that the goalposts have been shifting further and further away since the D'Oliveira affair in 1968. From personal experience I know that the Test and County Cricket Board has gradually given ground. They – or rather the MCC – resisted pressure from the South Africans in 1968 and they also stood up to pressure from Guyana in 1981, sticking to the vital principle that no-one should be able to tell the cricket authorities who can and cannot play.

When the Guyanese tried to ban England bowler Robin Jackman because of his South African links the Test was called off. But later that same year the Board began to waiver in the face of Mrs Gandhi's posturing before the 1981–2 tour of India. She said that the Northamptonshire captain and opener Geoff Cook and I would not be admitted unless we publicly renounced apartheid and stated that we would not go to South Africa again. George Mann, then chairman of the Test and County Cricket Board, and *Sunday Times* cricket writer Robin Marlar, whose presence came as a big surprise to me, attempted to put pressure on me through my solicitor friend Duncan Mutch, claiming that if I did not agree to Mrs Gandhi's terms the tour would have to be called off. They put the responsibility on me, which was very unfair, but I refused to comment. I reasoned that I had the right to go anywhere I chose and that if I surrendered they would want more from me next time. I had made it clear more than once that I hated apartheid, so I did not see the need to go any further. So far as I was concerned, Mrs Gandhi and her advisers had got themselves on the hook and it was up to them to get off it without my help. I had been planning a holiday in Hong Kong, staying with a friend, and just before I left the Test and County Cricket Board Secretary Donald Carr telephoned me, breathless and worried. 'Geoffrey, you're not thinking of going to South Africa on holiday before the tour of India, are you?' he asked.

I enjoyed playing Carr along, so I asked why he should be concerned about my private arrangements. He suggested that the Indians might regard my holidaying in South Africa as provocative, adding: 'They are very sensitive.' I pointed out in return that the Test and County Cricket Board had made a big issue out of protecting the rights of individuals to do whatever they wished. In fact, Carr and Mann had made it public that cricketers going to South Africa to coach, play or take a holiday would be supported so long as they were not part of any team. 'Are you saying that is no longer true?' I enquired innocently. Carr ummed and ahhed, coughed and spluttered and said hesitantly: 'Oh, no. It's just that they may see things differently.' I informed him that if I wanted to go to South Africa I would do so, and that I would not be held to ransom or party to any under-the-counter deals. Carr resorted to a lot of moral blackmail which amounted to 'Yes, you're right to do what you want, but the Indians may not think the same way.' I regarded that as blackmail, but eventually I put him out of his misery and told him exactly where I was going.

Subsequently, when our unofficial trip to South Africa had got under way, the Test and County Cricket Board again tried blackmail, stating that we had split international cricket into two camps – black and white. They argued that we would damage the livelihood of every professional cricketer in the country by reducing the number of tours and Tests. This in turn, they claimed, would reduce the income of the county clubs and force them to sack staff or stop recruiting. The next step was to announce that after we had received our three-year Test bans for the South African venture we were not to be chosen for county games against the Indian tourists that summer as it might offend the highly sensitive Indians. Yet they

147

persisted in saying they would back us if we went to South Africa as individuals. Thus the English counties became the first to bow to pressure and from that point on it was only a matter of time before the Test and County Cricket Board abandoned the vital principle of not allowing others to determine who they did or did not select for England.

The timetable of shame took in 1986, when Graham Gooch was hassled in the West Indies; 1988, when the Test and County Cricket Board warned all cricketers that if they went to coach or play in South Africa, even in a private capacity, they might jeopardize their international prospects; and finally 1988-9. This was the period in which India decided only to accept those players who publicly stated they would never play cricket in South Africa. It was a monstrous demand from a government trying to take the lead among the Third World countries. Once England refused to give in, the tour had to be cancelled, yet India was content to come to England in 1990! The Indians, who are all too ready to adopt threatening poses, should look at the apartheid in their own back yard, where discrimination on the grounds of race is common. Life for many Indians is much worse than it is for most blacks in South Africa. The West Indians actually put a ludicrous proposal on the agenda for the International Cricket Conference, suggesting that if any country objected to a player in a touring team he should be replaced by someone more acceptable. On that basis, we could have objected to Viv Richards and his battery of fast bowlers! How absurd!!

In the circumstances, I do not think that South Africa can expect any fairer treatment in the foreseeable future, and I believe they would be well advised to stop talking to either the Test and County Cricket Board or the International Cricket Conference. The black countries will never relax their sanctions until there is one-man, one-vote in South Africa, and perhaps not even then, and the white nations do not have the resolve to challenge the status quo. Doug Insole was at least honest when he told the South Africans:

'I'm not helping you. My job is to protect English cricket.' The South Africans have to face the fact that it will take a long time to get back into the fold of international cricket, even if they stop all unofficial tours and press forward as quickly as possible with reforms.

I remain convinced, however, that if Pamensky had taken my advice in 1982, South African cricket would not be in the mess it is today. I advised him to follow in the footsteps of Kerry Packer; to buy most, if not all, of the best players in the world; and to challenge world cricket head on. Perhaps if they had been successful in their efforts to recruit Ian Botham things would have been different. If the South Africans had captured the leading youngsters, the ones starting to make an impact on the Test scene, they would have been in a very strong bargaining position, just as Packer was. He approached the task of undermining the establishment with a single-minded determination and beat them into submission. The South African Cricket Union started down the same path; but then got lost. By giving five-year playing and coaching contracts to the cream of the world's cricketers the South Africans would have made their domestic Currie Cup competition the best. Whatever the agitators and demonstrators think, there will always be a supply of talent ready and willing to take the South African gold and forget about the shadow of possible Test bans.

9

Captain Boycott

I dedicated most of my life to cricket, realizing from the earliest days as a very ambitious youngster that nothing comes easily. It was in the accepted order of things that I should want to become captain of Yorkshire, for most boys in the country with any interest in cricket are brought up to regard that position as something special, an honour to be cherished. Nonetheless, there are times when I wish I had turned down the Yorkshire captaincy when it was offered to me during the 1970 tour of Australia.

I enjoyed the challenge of using my brains and my knowledge of cricket to plan as a game unfolded, but there is no doubt that taking up the leadership of the Yorkshire team harmed me a great deal. In the first instance, my troubles with the committee saddened me. I did not go to them asking for the captaincy, they offered the job to me. Unfortunately, the decision to appoint me as successor to Brian Close was not unanimous, and those who opposed it never fell into line with the majority. They found it easier to blame me for Yorkshire's failures than to accept the fact that we no longer had a very good side. Some wanted the return of an amateur captain; others saw an alternative to me in Richard Hutton, a former Cambridge blue.

Joe Lister, the Yorkshire secretary, took the opportunity to push that line when John Callaghan replaced Bill Bowes as cricket correspondent of the *Yorkshire Evening Post* in 1974. Lister took him on one side and indicated: 'You can do yourself a lot of good with the committee if you help create a climate in which we can get rid of Boycott as captain and bring in Hutton.' That sort of pressure from within the club, and pressure from the media put an extra burden on my batting. The national press was ready to run any story which carried my name at the drop of the proverbial hat, and the journalists were not too worried about getting the facts right. They operated from a distance and wrote anything which they thought would make an eye-catching headline.

In the early 1970s I was the best batsman in England and one of the best in the world. That is not conceit or arrogance. It is a statement of fact, which can be checked easily enough in Wisden and I do not think even my worst enemy would challenge my assertion. For a while as captain I played magnificently, becoming the first English batsman to average more than 100 in an English season when I managed 100.12 in 1971. The bulk of the Yorkshire membership rejoiced, yet Fred Trueman and a group of committee-men accused me of playing for myself. They seemed to take no account of the fact that in the last match of the season, when I got the 124 not out I needed for a three-figure average, Yorkshire beat Northamptonshire by an innings in two days.

I felt at the time that the better I played the better it would be for the team, and that if I put a lot of effort into the captaincy people might begin to give me the benefit of the doubt. Things did not work out that way. The captaincy troubles grew and Yorkshire continued to struggle. It became clear that each time I went out to the middle I was batting for my job, and it was like batting with a sack of coal on my back. Anyone who has attempted to carry a heavy burden over any length of time will realize what I mean. It does not seem too bad initially, but gradually it gets heavier and heavier and the person concerned begins to stagger under the weight.

I did my best to give an adventurous lead in those early days. I compiled a century as Yorkshire successfully chased 267 in 170 minutes against Warwickshire, and I shared in a match-winning stand with John Hampshire as we made 212 in less than three hours to beat Middlesex. There was also 233 out of 421–4 at Colchester, where Essex had to follow on and narrowly escaped defeat. I scored briskly enough in the Sunday League, notably in 1973 when, thanks largely to the runs provided by Hampshire and me, Yorkshire finished runners-up to Kent.

But there was always somebody finding fault. Thus I did become more defensive, partly because a lot of matches had to be saved before we could think of winning them. Every comparison shows that Yorkshire in my early years as captain scored more quickly and picked up more batting bonus points when I played, and I think it is very sad that some will remember me only as a match saver. That is just not true, and I know that research will show that I contributed significantly to nearly every Yorkshire championship victory over the decade. I accept that those who saw me only from my late thirties on will recall the dedicated technician, but cricket followers with longer memories will also remember a more classical player, who at times could and did dominate bowling attacks.

It would have been much easier for me to let others shoulder the responsibility of decision-making while I got on with the job of accumulating runs for Yorkshire and England, and I wish I had had the foresight of Herbert Sutcliffe, who declined his invitation to captain the county in 1927. Sutcliffe concentrated his mind on the job he did best. Because I loved Yorkshire cricket so much I became emotionally involved, and emotion clouds the judgement, making it difficult to think straight.

It caused me to opt out of international cricket for three years between 1974 and 1977 when I wanted to prove that I could make a good job of leading Yorkshire. Things actually improved when I was not on Test duty and available all the time, and in 1975 the county finished second in the championship. But I should have realized that being captain of the county did not really matter; my batting was far more important. The truth is that great batsmen, great bowlers and great wicketkeepers have far more influence on the game and are remembered when captains have long been forgotten. Captains come and go, some good, others bad, most of them insignificant. Ray Illingworth, Mike Brearley and Australia's Richie Benaud may be exceptions, but the majority are just names. It is the exploits of batsmen, bowlers and wicketkeepers that capture the imagination, cram the pages of the record books and live on in the minds of the public.

With the benefit of hindsight, one can argue that the fates conspired to give Sir Leonard Hutton the best of both worlds. He was snubbed by Yorkshire and passed over for the captaincy, yet he became the first professional captain of England and enjoyed great success in that role. He probably never knew just how lucky he had been in not having to face the daily difficulties that beset a county captain. I would certainly have much preferred to captain only England, for that would have been easier, with better players on hand, players chosen by me. Hutton was spared the routine chores of dealing with the county committee, of encouraging moderate players, of making sure that the travel and hotel arrangements were in order. Hutton could concentrate on his batting and turn his attentions to captaincy during only five weeks of the summer, while on tour with the England team he could leave a lot to the manager and take a match off when necessary to recharge his batteries. I am sure there would have been an inquest if I had taken a match off when leading Yorkshire, who seemed to want a superman in charge.

Interestingly, this is another area in which England continues to get things wrong. It would never consider making anyone captain who did not already do the job for his county, yet in one way it is asking the impossible. It is ridiculous to expect a star player to maintain an exceptionally high level of performance while captaining both his county and his country. Benaud, Illingworth and Brearley may all have been pretty good cricketers – certainly the first two were – but not one of them was ever the outstanding player in the team, so they could all give a bit more thought to the problems of leadership. A top-class batsman or bowler makes too many demands on himself mentally and physically to leave much to spare. He cannot do the thinking for others and, if he attempts to look after everything, he will wear himself down.

As much as I care for Yorkshire, I now realize it would have been better for me to have declined the captaincy. I would have been better off without that distraction over so many years, although I doubt whether the county would have done any better under a different leader. For twenty years the team has not been good enough, and none of my successors, Hampshire, Chris Old, Illingworth, David Bairstow and Phil Carrick, has succeeded in overcoming this.

The most constant factor has been the fantastic support of the Yorkshire members and supporters. They gave me an inner strength when I felt badly let down and betrayed by the Yorkshire committee and without them I often felt that I would have been better off with another county. Not everyone has been on my side, which was only to be expected, but a large majority stood by me through some dark times.

The loss of the captaincy at the end of the 1978 season still came as a bitter disappointment because it appeared that I had been blamed for all that had gone wrong. I would have liked the chance to work with Illingworth, who began his term as team manager in the same year. I believed then that the idea of linking the captain with a team manager had considerable merit. We had previously got on very well together, and when captain of England, he often asked my opinion, one notable occasion being the Lord's Test against New Zealand in 1969. He won the toss on a very dark morning and there was a good deal of debate about what to do. The pitch, grassy and with a ridge at the far end, looked mottled at the pavilion end, where it felt dry and not too firm. None of the England batsmen wanted to bat first on the ridge and Illingworth asked me what I thought. I told him that I personally did not want to bat on the ridge, but that I would do so if I were captain. 'Our batsmen won't like it, but I think Derek Underwood will bowl them out very cheaply as the dry end wears and allows plenty of turn,' I told him. He took my advice and we batted. The third ball of the day from Dick Motz removed me for nought – caught in the gulley from one that I did not 'pick up' out of the dark Lord's pavilion. As I dejectedly marched through the silent Long Room and climbed the stairs to the dressing-room a chap stopped me and demanded: 'What did you get out for? I've come six thousand miles from South Africa to see you bat.' I did well to keep my cool. I looked at him and said: 'Well, I'll tell you one thing, I didn't get out on purpose.' Having given me time to 'come round', Illingworth made a point of thanking me for helping him to make a difficult decision.

He probably needed some moral support as England slumped to 63–5 in the morning session, but my conviction that he had done the right thing never wavered. We eventually made 190 and 340 and New Zealand, who replied with 169 and 131, were beaten by 230 runs, Underwood finishing with match figures of 11–70. The Kent left-armer proved almost unplayable in the second innings with 7–32, while Glenn Turner became the youngest player to bat through a completed Test innings, making an unbeaten 43.

Then, in 1970, Illingworth asked me who I thought was the best fast bowler in England behind John Snow and Alan Ward. He had already earmarked this pair for the tour to Australia in the winter and I advised him to take Peter Lever, from Lancashire, who swung the ball out at a lively pace and was a great-hearted trier with plenty of stamina. Illingworth put him to the test in the last game between England and the Rest of the World, when he justified my faith in him by taking seven wickets. I also encouraged Illingworth to take Lever's Lancashire colleague, Ken Shuttleworth, who was not so easy to communicate with and needed careful handling, but who could be a very good bowler.

Subsequently during the tour Illingworth often visited my room to sound me out and I helped him a lot with Snow. The Sussex paceman often appeared difficult because he had a lazy streak, so Illingworth asked me to 'gee him up' a bit. I got into the habit of needling Snow. 'When are you going to let one or two go and bowl quick?' I would ask. 'You'll never get anyone out bowling at medium pace,' I would say on other occasions. Snowy got quite mad and usually gave me a mouthful in return, but my tactics did the trick. The rest of the batsmen were a bit wary of upsetting Snow, well aware that all fast bowlers have long memories and that he would be bowling at them in the following championship season. I was never afraid of him, although I respected his ability.

By the time Illingworth returned to Yorkshire in 1979 our paths had taken us along different routes and we had seen very little of each other. In the circumstances, I am sure he had developed preconceived ideas about the situation at the club, taking too much notice of the rumours and the stories in the more sensational newspapers. There is no doubt in my mind that he was instrumental in getting rid of me as captain, because as the new manager he was in a position to make demands. The Yorkshire committee could hardly appoint him and then tie his hands over such an important issue as the captaincy.

He wanted total control and presumably saw me as an obstacle. I believe that if he had worked with me instead of trying to establish his authority over the subsequent captains, Hampshire and Old, we could have brought about a significant improvement.

We understood the Yorkshire way of playing cricket, having been brought up in the same school. Losing hurt both of us. Illingworth could have kept the committee off my back, maintained discipline in the dressing-room while I was out in the middle batting, and helped me to think for the others. Most important, we respected each other as cricketers.

At the start of the 1979 season, Illingworth called me into his office and said that he wanted me to go out and bat like the great player I was, telling me to 'relax and forget about the captaincy'. This was music to my ears. I went on to score 1,538 runs for an average of 102.53, but Yorkshire did not do too well and the whispering began again in the corners. As far as I could tell, a popular theory among the committee was that if I scored fewer runs the team would prosper. I could not make any sense of anything that was going on. When the results were unsatisfactory under my captaincy I took the blame as a poor leader. When the results were poor under a different captain it was still my fault because I should have made fewer runs! The reasoning defied analysis, for logic indicated that Yorkshire would have lost a lot of games much more easily if I had not defied the opposition bowling. My personal success upset a section of the committee, some of whom even indicated that they thought I had averaged over 100 just to make them look foolish – as if they needed any assistance!

Not surprisingly, in 1980 I found myself back where I started, wary and cautious of all that was taking place behind the scenes. Talk of new blood, of exciting young prospects, filled the air. As ever, I felt I was batting for my job.

Illingworth left in the spring of 1984, and Brian Close took over as cricket chairman. I knew that it was only a matter of time before Close, aided by Bryan Stott and Phil Sharpe, got rid of me. It all seems such a waste now. I could have achieved so much more for the Yorkshire club they all claimed to care so much about if I had been given whole-hearted support. Any doubts nursed by the committee should have been brought out into the open and dealt with in frank discussions. That, surely, is what democracy and fair play are all about.

I am sorry that Brian Sellers did not remain as cricket chairman when I took over the captaincy, for he had the strength and character that was lacking in so many others. He had no favourites and said all he had to say to your face. He spoke a language that everyone understood and backed his captain and players without fear or favour. Sellers knew that personal feelings should not be allowed to affect his judgements, so it did not matter whether he liked you. He treated all who crossed his path the same way.

Sellers, of course, had mastered the most tricky part of captaincy – man-management. A good captain needs to be skilful in dealing with committees, players and the press. It is astonishing how administrators expect young men to have all the necessary qualifications at a comparatively early age without any formal training. The average county cricketer is coached from the age of nine or ten on the basics of batting, bowling and fielding, yet captaincy is supposed to be second nature or something that an individual picks up along the way. Sometimes that is the case and there are some natural leaders, but generally a cricketer finds it very hard to step up from the ranks and take overall responsibility for running the team. He endures the agonies of sleepless nights, arguments and disagreements, and his own form usually suffers.

While commerce and industry spend huge sums on management training, sport relies on the old hit-and-miss system. I wish I had attended under my own steam an organization like MAST – Management and Skills Training. I did not know then that such courses were available and I don't suppose many cricketers are aware of their existence today. This is another area in which English cricket could help itself and it would not cost the counties very much to set up some sort of winter school for potential captains. Obviously some would do much better than others, but that is the case with batting and bowling too, and leadership is an important skill. Interestingly, Humphrey Walters, who runs MAST, was encouraged to start his company by Brearley, the one England captain in recent times to demonstrate great ability in dealing with people.

Logic, however, is only one factor in the captaincy equation. In my case an emotional involvement with Yorkshire cricket left me with a blind spot. Because I so much wanted the team to be successful and to make a personal success of the captaincy I found it impossible to stand back and be objective. Had I done so, I might have accepted that I had limited material with which to work. With the benefit of hindsight, I can say with absolute certainty that the only team to captain is a good team; if you have ten skilful and experienced players under you then there is likely to be no problem. On the other hand, if you captain a poor team there is endless worry and heartache. Similarly, captaincy is straightforward when things are running smoothly, but it becomes a full-time occupation as soon as anything goes wrong.

It is easier for a moderate player to throw himself totally into the role of captain, as he is involved only marginally out in the middle as batsman or bowler. He can channel all his thoughts and energies in one direction; to achieve a distinction otherwise unattainable to him.

The other side of the coin is that captaining an unsuccessful team can tarnish a player's reputation through no fault of his own. A great player can control his own destiny. But a captain's fate is inevitably in the hands of others.

10

Trouble up north

Yorkshire cricket found itself in a terrible mess at the end of the 1989 season and stumbled into another major controversy in the early weeks of 1990 as the president, Viscount Mountgarret, angrily stalked out of a committee meeting, refused to take a less active role and was replaced by Sir Leonard Hutton. The situation comes as no great surprise to anyone who has studied the administrative set-up. The Yorkshire committee comprises twenty-three representatives elected by seventeen administrative districts and they in turn serve on four sub-committees, namely: cricket; finance; grounds and membership; and public relations and fund-raising. The four chairmen of the sub-committees, elected by the general committee members, together with the president, treasurer and general committee chairman, form a management committee which has enjoyed far-reaching powers but which is destined to fill a less prominent role in the 1990s. In 1989 the club was dominated by three men with no in-depth knowledge of the game and one whose track record shows a long series of failures. Mountgarret, the general committee chairman

Brian Walsh and public relations chairman Sid Fielden have gained prominent positions without the experience or the background to fill them adequately; while cricket chairman Brian Close, although a gifted sportsman, never realized his full talent as a player and cannot concentrate his mind sufficiently to bring any real judgement to bear on the organization of the cricket.

Thus the four people at the heart of the once-great county's day-to-day operation were weak links. Like characters in one of those marvellously complex plays by Alan Ayckbourn they spent their time hurrying busily down blind alleys, dragging a poor committee in their wake. Additionally, they exerted a massive and largely misguided influence through the management committee. They should be prepared to shoulder a heavy burden of responsibility for the decline in Yorkshire's standing with both the leading officials of the Test and County Cricket Board at Lord's and a shrinking membership, weary of unfulfilled promises. Instead, club officials hide behind an endless string of excuses for poor performances on the field and poor facilities off it.

It gives me no satisfaction to see the club in such a mess, even though those in charge have so often attempted to make me the scapegoat. Indeed, I am saddened by all the obvious mistakes and extremely worried by the blank refusal of people such as Walsh and Close to even appreciate the size of the problem. They remain both defiant and defensive, so that any member of the committee who speaks out in an attempt to rectify matters needing urgent attention can expect to be marked down as a trouble-maker on the wrong side of a clear dividing line. This was roughly indicated by the way in which an individual was required to address the former president. The 'good boys' referred to him as Richard, the rest as My Lord. Inevitably, this latter group included me, along with Tony Vann, Peter Quinn, Philip Ackroyd, Tony Boot, Jack Sokell and Robert Hilliam – the so-called 'Boycott faction'.

Some individuals have found it easier to keep quiet and say nothing, passive baggage on a ship heading for the rocks. I understand their concern at being patronized and cajoled by Mountgarret and Walsh, who are good at that, if nothing else, but I cannot forgive their decision to sit back and hope for an easy ride. That has never been my way, and I cannot change. After thirty years in professional cricket, I am very much aware that honest opinions, expressed openly and constructively, are often unwelcome. You make enemies by speaking your mind, but I can live with that.

I am convinced that the members have no more than a sketchy idea of how badly things had been run. Very little information is given out through the press, although it represents the only link between the administration and the membership, which, after all, makes everything possible by providing a sound financial base. I have argued for many years that all committee meetings should be open to journalists, who could then make up their own minds and report accordingly.

Such a revolutionary suggestion did not exactly fall on deaf ears. On the contrary, it outraged the 'inner cabinet', who persist in thinking that they alone are capable of making decisions. Arthur Connell, who became the first chairman of the general committee in 1971, once said: 'We know what is good for the club, the members don't.' That struck me as a very arrogant and insulting attitude to take; I said so and earned yet another black mark. As a matter of record, the position of chairman came into being when the then president, Sir William Worsley, had trouble with his hearing and struggled to chair meetings. He had no hesitation in stepping down in the best interests of the county because he was that sort of man. He always put Yorkshire first; it is a pity that more people cannot follow his admirable example.

The power-base revolves around the central figures and you do not have to attend many committee meetings before the pattern becomes all too clear. The basic agreement centres on the principle that 'if you vote for me, I'll vote for you', so the ex-players put their weight behind Mountgarret, Walsh and Close. Bob Appleyard, Bryan Stott, Phil Sharpe and Bob Platt can be relied upon at all times to support Close and they in turn receive unquestioning backing from Walsh.

I discovered to my cost just how effective the system could be when Sir Kenneth Parkinson was president. I liked Sir Kenneth and enjoyed a happy relationship with him, but there is no doubt that he let me down, himself and, most important, Yorkshire cricket over the Northamptonshire incident in 1978, when John Hampshire staged a 'go-slow' with Colin Johnson and deliberately sacrificed a bonus point to make some sort of protest about my own scoring rate. Sir Kenneth, in the area on business, saw exactly what happened and privately promised me unqualified support, only to significantly shift his ground when quietly warned by committee strong-men that if he did not back the official line he would not be nominated by the committee for the presidency at the next annual meeting. Our paths crossed many times before his death in 1981 and he admitted that he had been wrong. Sadly it was too late.

Fielden can also be relied on to accept the cricket committee line without comment. It is no secret that, after being a close personal friend, he turned against me in a quite dramatic fashion to align himself with Close and Bob Appleyard. His motivation is self-preservation, too. Having come to prominence with the Old Reform Group and betrayed their trust, he knows that some people on the committee won't forgive or have confidence in him again, so he needs what amounts to protection from the cricket committee to retain his position as public relations chairman. At the same time, he is useful to them as an official spokesman and can be relied upon to say the right things from their point of view, making his mouth say anything that will keep him in favour.

This clique, hanging so desperately on to power, continually calls for unity. 'We must be united if we are to make progress,' they tell the world. What they really mean is that they want unity on their own terms. They expect all the members of the committee to fall in behind any idea they might put forward, whether it be good, bad or indifferent. Anyone who does so automatically becomes a nice person, the right type for the committee. Equally, opponents who want to express their views strongly are 'dangerous' and 'disloyal', words they trot out at every opportunity to create the impression to the public that Yorkshire's problems could be solved quickly if only they were given the chance. 'How can we make progress when we spend so much time arguing among ourselves?' they ask, and it sounds like a good question until you look below the surface. I would reply that nothing can be achieved without frank, open and, sometimes, heated debates and I say again: 'Let the press attend all committee meetings to make their own judgement.'

I know from first-hand experience that, among others, Tony Woodhouse, Raymond Clegg and Phil Sharpe hardly ever speak during committee meetings, so what contribution do they make? To my knowledge, Sharpe has spoken only twice in all the meetings I have attended, although he is ready to put up his hand to support his friends. The two 'crucial' topics he raised involved something connected with his duties as an England selector and a complaint from women members in York who felt that the membership regulations discriminated in favour of men. Although those are matters that should concern a district representative, I would have expected much more from a man with his experience of cricket.

The situation exposes one of the weaknesses in recording and publishing attendances at committee meetings. I attracted a lot of criticism when I concentrated on promoting my autobiography during 1987 and again later, in 1988, when I declined to waste my time at the public relations and fund-raising meetings held under the chairmanship of Fielden. I stood accused of neglecting my duties, yet others with a 100 per cent appearance record had contributed no more because they turned up and remained silent. They could have achieved the same result by sending cardboard cut-outs. The simple truth is that it suited Walsh and company to have Geoffrey Boycott out of the way. They would much rather lecture the cut-outs who do not mind a 'them and us' atmosphere.

I think I can claim to approach most subjects with an open mind. I have very fixed views about batting and don't listen too often to conflicting opinions in that field, but I am ready to debate an issue and even to argue a point fiercely. I feel, therefore, that if the committee really does care about Yorkshire and the mess the club is in, it should welcome the most heated exchanges. Instead, we have a one-way system. A case in point is the cricket academy at Bradford Park Avenue, which, while being a splendid idea, is certainly not an end in itself. I happen to think that it was not thought through properly in the formative stages. For one thing, the derelict Park Avenue ground is in the wrong place and, to be worthwhile, the academy needs to be much bigger, with at least twenty boys taking part. Although Bradford Council offered plenty of incentives, the academy is a costly venture for Yorkshire, £29,000 in the first year, so I feel that every step along the way should have been carefully discussed.

Business commitments took me out of the country to Australia when the academy discussion began, which left the way clear for the cricket committee 'experts' to steamroller through their plans. Close and Appleyard merely claimed that Headingley was totally unsuitable and that only Bradford could be used. Predictably, Sharpe, Stott and Platt fell into step as the ex-players marched along, dismissing opposition on the grounds that it was ill-informed. They put forward no hard evidence, being happy to rely entirely on their own opinions, which easily carried the day in my absence. When I returned, however, I took the trouble to investigate the possibilities for myself. I discovered immediately that at no stage had any talks been held with the owners, Leeds Cricket, Football and Athletic Club, to see if they were interested in accommodating the ground staff at Headingley, which made me question whether Close and Appleyard had fully investigated the potential of the two prospective venues, as they claimed to have done. In taking such a dogmatic stance, these two men had further damaged the fragile relationship between Yorkshire and its landlords at headquarters, although, it should be noted, they no doubt did themselves a lot of good with the members in Bradford, the district they both represent. They also upset Leeds City Council, with whom the county had established an excellent business, personal and profit-making relationship through the indoor school at Headingley. The Council learned of the academy 'informally', and the chairman of the Leisure Services Committee, Bernard Atha, wrote a stinging letter to Walsh, pointing out that 'any approach to the city in connection with developments at Headingley is hardly likely to receive a favourable reception if the academy is to move from its natural home.'

I felt that Close could no longer view this issue impartially, having agreed to become Chairman of The Friends of Park Avenue, a minor pressure group. As another split in the Yorkshire committee became public property, I put before them a fully reasoned case for the academy being in Leeds, based on the fact that Headingley stood at the centre of Yorkshire's activities. I challenged Close to name another county that ran its groundstaff away from headquarters. No reply! I underlined the advantages of Leeds, where the youngsters would have been able to join the first- and second-team players at practice sessions, thus gaining valuable experience, and see some first-class cricket. They would also have been available to help out during the Test matches and take part in a busy indoor school programme. The only counter-thrust from Close and Appleyard concerned the supposed shortage of net facilities at Headingley, yet they had not taken the trouble to mention this to the groundsman Keith Boyce, who assured me that he envisaged no problems in this direction. The weight of evidence piled up against Bradford, but still the vote went in its favour, a decision soon followed by talk of taking first-class cricket back to Park Avenue. The real motives of the Bradford lobby were now fully exposed.

Ironically, behind all these brick walls cemented into place by self-interest, Mountgarret and Walsh fought a long and bitter struggle for power. While claiming to unite Yorkshire in public, they aspired to each other's role behind the scenes. Walsh used the theme 'I can handle the president' throughout his campaign for the chairmanship, exploiting the well-known fact that Mountgarret helped to drive out Reg Kirk, who took the chair after the 1984 election landslide for the Reform Group.

Walsh must have misjudged his man, for this did not turn out to be the case. He and Mountgarret were usually to be seen in the comparative privacy of the committee room locked in combat as they tore in to each other. It was a sorry spectacle, the end-product of Mountgarret's vision of himself as a latter-day Lord Hawke, moulding Yorkshire cricket to his personal design. He possesses none of Hawke's qualities, so he continued to chase the rainbow of his ambition, sublimely unaware that he was by no means first choice when Yorkshire sought a replacement for the previous president Norman Yardley. The former county and England captain had resigned in 1984, reacting honourably to a crushing vote of no-confidence in the com-mittee which had awarded me a testimonial and followed it with the sack. It had been his intention to move quietly into the background as president and he was making the necessary moves to reduce the power of the office when he stood down.

I initially approached Lord Hanson on behalf of the county as Kirk spent some sleepless nights searching through the list of members. I had done Lord Hanson a small favour by appearing in an advertising montage which he used for his companies in America and England

and I subsequently came into contact with him again when he agreed to help with some advertising in my testimonial brochure in 1984. Yardley had resigned in January and it occurred to me that a businessman of Lord Hanson's international standing would make the perfect successor. He gave careful thought to the possibility after Kirk had followed up my original talks officially, and indicated that if he accepted he would want, as he put it, 'a man on the board'. At that time the facility existed to meet that condition and Sir Gordon Linacre, chairman of Yorkshire Post Newspapers, was Lord Hanson's nominee, but he finally decided that, as he lived for half the year in the United States, he could not fill the vacancy.

Marcus Worsley and Sir James Hill were other prominent people considered before Mountgarret, who promptly declared his intention of actively involving himself in just about everything. He saw no virtue in becoming a figure-head. This approach threw him straight into a complicated political situation for which he was ill-equipped, and his attempts to impose his will on events steered the club into troubled waters.

Mountgarret felt slighted if he was not involved in everything and, for example, attended Test and County Cricket Board meetings at Lord's with secretary Joe Lister, even though it is custom and practice for the chairman to represent the county. What he did not realize was that he could not be taken seriously by men steeped in cricket. Possibly because he felt threatened by his chairman Walsh, the president made strenuous and undignified efforts to become chairman as well as president after an embarrassing annual meeting at the Queen's Hotel in Leeds in 1989. This was postponed from the original date when notice did not reach the bulk of the members in time and, while Lister shouldered the blame and indicated a willingness to meet some of the extra expense incurred out of his own pocket, many on the committee said that Walsh had delayed the process of distributing all the literature. His protracted discussions with the proposers and seconders of several resolutions left Lister with a tight schedule. Mountgarret hinted at this in a letter to one of the members who forced the postponement, Maurice Cooper, and subsequently threw Walsh to the wolves when the meeting eventually took place. Having contacted a number of committee-men, urging them to put forward his name as chairman, Mountgarret appeared to be in a strong position when Walsh wilted under vigorous cross-examination by Giles Firbank. His apparent inability to answer difficult questions and extra pressure from Mountgarret to explain his conduct left him ashen-faced and his blustering created a very poor impression. Many observers left the meeting convinced that he would be replaced.

When it came to the crunch things did not work out as Mountgarret expected. There is always a full committee meeting as soon as practicable after the annual meeting to elect the various sub-committees, as well as the chairman, and in 1989 Stott, as usual, proposed Walsh. This was perfectly normal under the agreement which kept the chosen few in positions of authority, but then the president's name was put forward for chairman and a tremendous row broke out. The treasurer intervened, saying that in his opinion it would not be a good thing for Mountgarret to be both president and chairman, while David Welch, from Rotherham, added his weight to that line of reasoning. Welch does not speak often, but what he says counts for a lot and he described the president's position as 'monstrous', presumably being well aware of all the lobbying that had been done. Walsh, meanwhile, said that he would not stand against the president, which may sound quite noble. I don't think it was. He seemed to me not to want to run the risk of being defeated, although he did not duck away from the fight when he thought he had a good chance of beating Kirk in 1984 and 1985.

Walsh's position had been further strengthened by some 'horse trading' behind the scenes. As a Leeds member he had put himself in opposition to Close and

Appleyard as they pushed their academy scheme at Bradford and at one stormy committee meeting he declined to continue the business until Appleyard apologized and withdrew a suggestion that he was biased in favour of his home district. A campaign was quietly conducted with the sole aim of getting rid of Walsh as chairman and, according to some members of the committee, he was 'dead and buried' on the day of the annual meeting. That day, however, Stott and Eric Houseman, the representative for Harrogate, held a private meeting with Walsh and persuaded him to give full backing to Bradford in return for support as chairman. This about-face altered the balance of power, although Mountgarret, unaware of developments, pressed on with his plans the following day and was caught on the wrong foot when strong opposition to his 'takeover' materialized.

In the end, Mountgarret withdrew and an uneasy peace reigned briefly. When Walsh announced his re-election as chairman to the press, he was specifically asked: 'Was there any opposition?' Now Walsh thinks he is very smart with words and regards himself as something of a humourist, so he replied: 'Only from my wife, who would like me to be at home more often.' This was somewhat different from the reality of the situation: Walsh made no mention of the fact that Mountgarret's name had been put forward to replace him as chairman, nor that the opposition to his re-election was so strong that he came within a whisker of being unseated.

Mountgarret kept his powder dry, preferring to bide his time and let Walsh damage himself at least in the eyes of those on the inside, but these two leading figures never came close to the sort of harmony they demanded so often from others. Driven on by their conflicting desires to win friends and direct the course of events, they pulled this way and that, their serious differences surfacing at Scarborough. The captain, Phil Carrick, motivated by a run of dreadful results and unsatisfactory performances, finally decided the moment had come for him to enter the ring. He wrote to all members of the general committee expressing deep concern about Yorkshire's prospects unless there was a change of policy. At the same time, a group of senior players put pen to paper to express similar sentiments on their own behalf, addressing their letter to Close and Walsh rather than to Mountgarret. All this unrest came to a head towards the end of the season, demonstrating once more that the cricket committee, who were caught unawares, were out of touch. Indeed, the fact that Carrick went over the heads of the ex-players on the cricket committee he worked alongside and sat in committee with indicated just how little faith he had in them. Eventually Close, Walsh and Lister met Carrick, David Bairstow, Ashley Metcalfe, Kevin Sharp, Paul Jarvis, Martyn Moxon, Arnie Sidebottom, Stuart Fletcher and Richard Blakey, but not before Mountgarret had embarked on another of his telephone marathons, trying to persuade members of the committee that he should be asked to take part. 'As president, I have the right to be involved with everything,' he insisted to anyone who would listen, and this led to a row in the sponsors' tent at North Marine Road. He could hardly have chosen a worse place, as the Scarborough Festival is a popular attraction, drawing big crowds, and the angry exchanges with Close did not escape attention.

This pantomime before an amused if puzzled audience confirmed my theory that Mountgarret wanted to wield absolute power in the club. As a member of the House of Lords, he seems to me to retain a feudal attitude, regarding a wide range of people as inferior, to be used as and when he sees fit. In the circumstances, the president was not the best of negotiators, as we discovered when he took over as Yorkshire's spokesman and chief negotiator in talks with the Leeds club regarding the Headingley lease. As is reasonably well known, they own the Headingley ground and are principally concerned with running one of the most famous Rugby League clubs in the world. Yorkshire, for their part, pay a rent to use the cricket section and, while the arrangement worked well enough in the past, it is generally acknowledged that the two bodies have drifted apart.

Mountgarret asked the committee to trust him, to let him negotiate and secure better terms from Leeds Cricket, Football and Athletic Club. Matters drifted along until suddenly, out of the blue, he calmly informed the committee that nothing more could be done. The owners, he said, had not been helpful and Yorkshire would have to make the best of things.

It did not emerge until much later that Leeds Cricket, Football and Athletic Club, as a final gesture on the part of their chairman Norman Shuttleworth, had put forward a business proposition. The details came from the *Yorkshire Evening Post*, not the president. Yorkshire, it transpired, could have taken over control of the cricket side at Headingley, but Mountgarret, Walsh and the treasurer decided that the project involved too great a risk. They were frightened by the sums of money – £250,000 as a basic annual rental plus probably another £120,000 in maintenance – and the idea required both careful thought and detailed analysis. Fair enough, but the full Yorkshire committee, the elected representatives of the seventeen districts, should have made the final decision after taking into account all the factors. Instead, we remained in the dark until the local press did the job that should have been no more than routine for Mountgarret.

The president never received any mandate to assume overall responsibility and make independent decisions on such a massive scale and subsequently it began to look as if he had made a mistake. Yorkshire is on a slippery downhill slope at best and comparison with the fortunes of the 'old enemy' from across the Pennines shows the club in an increasingly poor light. Lancashire, benefiting from owning its own ground at Old Trafford, declared a profit of £306,000 for 1989, while Yorkshire managed a miserable £76,000 and was forced to tighten its belt. Bearing in mind those statistics, Yorkshire ought to have looked more closely into the Leeds offer. Advertising boards produce an income in excess of £350,000 and rising, plus £50,000 from corporate hospitality, but all this must have been lost on Mountgarret, who, when pressed by me, merely muttered about the need for confidentiality to avoid leaks and made a grudging apology for not being more open. This hardly made sense since the press broke the news anyway. I told the president that it is impossible to defend democracy through dictatorship.

When Vivien Stone, a Leeds member, saw the story in the *Yorkshire Evening Post* she tackled Walsh, who told her the paper was misinformed. Such replies cannot be excused on any grounds; they reveal a disregard for the people who should matter most to club officials – the members. It is a members' club, although you might not think so from the way they are treated. Over the years they have been abused as the faces of government changed while the policies stayed the same.

Walsh initially refused to call a meeting on 10 October to talk about the sorry state of the cricket. His head was so deep in the sand that he failed to appreciate the significance of the letter he and every other member of the committee had received from Carrick. As this correspondence is so important, it is useful in terms of setting the scene to understand just how far the captain wanted to go. He wrote as follows:

> I need remind no-one on the general committee that the current season has turned out to be an extremely disappointing one for all concerned. There have been several mitigating factors: poor batting form in the early half of the season and serious injury to two important bowlers which have kept them out for the whole season, plus injuries to many other key players who have spent lengthy spells out of the team.

The plain truth is that, even with a full squad of players, we just about compete with other more progressive counties, as 1987 proved. Any injury at all to key players proves that with our Yorkshire-born policy, we do not compete on level terms and always have our backs to the wall. The other sixteen counties either import overseas players or sign England cricketers who will complement their existing staff.

Whether we like it or not, sponsorship is the life-blood of cricket these days and we will not add to our list of sponsors or retain existing ones unless we are seen to be successful and progressing. Repeated failure cannot be the right image for companies who put their marketing and advertising budget into our club. They obviously want to be associated with success.

There is nothing that I and the other Yorkshire players would like more than Yorkshire to win competitions with a team composed solely of Yorkshiremen. But, realistically, this is not going to happen and I believe that the time has come for the committee of this club to take stock of the situation and relax its Yorkshire-born only policy. May I suggest that you should decide in future that we play a minimum of eight Yorkshire-born players and allow three outside signings to complement our existing players. There are players of the highest quality around who would strengthen our team and could bring some refreshing ideas into Yorkshire cricket.

This is a decision that you as a committee should take without asking the membership, who no doubt would reject the idea once again – you should give a positive lead. Some members will resign if this course of action is taken, but we have to be forward-looking and interest younger people in the club. The membership is ageing and there are very few young members around. Success will attract them. There is another point that I think you should consider. The Yorkshire players of today are not generally steeped in the history of the club and perhaps do not feel tied to it in the same way as their predecessors did. The better members of the team who attract attention from other counties are not going to remain with Yorkshire for ever if they are unable to reap the benefits of success.

They will be tempted to move on to the success-ful and progressive counties who can offer greater financial security. I ask you to consider these points not because I am indifferent to Yorkshire, but because, like you, I care passionately about it and am concerned about tomorrow. The time has come to grasp the nettle and replace the unwritten rule which limits us to Yorkshire-born players only by a written rule which stipulates the minimum number that will play. Let us preserve our identity by all means, but let us make the adjustments required which will once again set this club back among the front-runners in English cricket.

Such strong sentiments, obviously the product of much heart-searching, should have sounded some alarm-bells and demanded an immediate response. Predictably, little happened, even though the senior players made it crystal clear to cricket chairman Close and club chairman Walsh when they met them that they took no great pride in playing for Yorkshire. The unmistakable message was in fact that the players put financial reward at the head of their priorities. It was against this background that Walsh resisted for as long as he could demands for a crisis meeting of the full committee. Mountgarret seized on the opportunity, pushing and prodding eight committee-men to contact the club chairman with calls for action. The president wanted rid of Walsh and it could not be helped if Close had to be sacrificed along the way. Poor results meant that the cricket chairman, too, became increasingly vulnerable as 1989 wore on. Mountgarret telephoned Vann, Quinn and Tony Roberts, and persuaded Roberts to put his request for a meeting in writing. Remarkably, in view of his track record, Mountgarret, who has not exactly been a friend of mine, told Vann: 'We must bring about a change of direction. Walsh has to go. I would support Geoff Boycott as cricket chairman and so would Roberts.'

On top of three or four calls to Vann the president pestered Quinn, once getting him out of bed at half past midnight. He told both of them that he could not 'co-exist with Walsh for another day'. He further admitted that the cricket committee had made a mess of things and that he feared rumblings throughout the winter from the members. An agitated shadow of the confident man who stood before his first annual meeting waving a cricket bat and trumpeting that he stood for unity and a common sense of purpose, he said to Quinn: 'I suppose GB detests me more than anyone in the world, but it is time to have a new cricket chairman and a new chairman of the club. Do you think Boycott would take the cricket chairmanship?' Roberts, who has no connection with the Reform Group or, for that matter, with me, contacted Quinn. 'When are we going to get a new cricket chairman?' he asked. All this activity could not be dismissed as coincidence. The president had gone into the munitions factory and produced a lot of bullets which he hoped his press-ganged infantry would fire. In doing so, he fooled nobody but himself. His determination to play politics caused havoc, although Walsh and the rest of the committee knew what he was doing. Endless disruption ensued at the committee meetings, with people watching to see which way the president would go. Would there be official support for Walsh while the knife plunged into his back, or would the animosity be out in the open? In short,

Mountgarret established a reputation as a wheeler-dealer and, as he did so, set the tone for the level of behaviour throughout the club.

To a large extent, therefore, he dug his own grave. A lot of committee members were fed up with him by the time they gathered at Headingley on 17 January 1990 to consider the agenda for the annual meeting. Unavoidably delayed, I arrived some twenty minutes after the start to find Mountgarret and Townend in the corridor outside the committee room. It was the same place in which I had waited in 1986 while the committee decided to sack me. When I joined my committee colleagues I could hardly believe the groundswell of opinion against Mountgarret, with Fielden and Tony Cawdry, from Halifax, leading the calls to either curb his activities or get rid of him altogether. The overwhelming consensus of opinion was that Mountgarret could not be allowed to go on doing exactly as he pleased, but, to avoid bad publicity, a majority on the committee were prepared to renominate him as president on the understanding that he did not interfere on a day-to-day basis. When this proposal was put to him, Mountgarret would have none of it. He was not prepared to discuss the position. When he had left, Fielden said he was ready with another name, but I argued successfully that we should wait for at least a couple of days to give Mountgarret time to think. Although I had no time for him, I felt the committee should act responsibly and not rush into anything. Mountgarret, clearly rattled, allowed himself to be quoted freely in the press the next day, leaving the committee with the deep-seated suspicion that he had taken the first step to publicize the rift in the hope of rallying members to his side. After that there could be no turning back and Sir Leonard was persuaded to allow his name to go forward. When the committee met the following Sunday, 21 January, to officially nominate Sir Leonard, Appleyard proposed that they should apologize to Mountgarret for keeping him waiting outside the committee-room while the presidency was discussed. I opposed that idea. The committee had never bothered about such niceties when sacking players, nor when they ended my playing career, and in any case it is standard practice in any organization for a person to leave the room when he is being considered for office.

Mountgarret's activities might not have been so harmful in the shadow of a stronger, better chairman, who could have kept him firmly in his place. It is Yorkshire's ill-fortune, therefore, that Walsh is cast in the same mould. He enjoys the chairmanship for the prestige it brings him and for the high profile he can maintain. He loves to have his picture in the newspapers and to appear on television. It seemed very much in character in November 1989 when he persuaded all the members of the committee not to take part in a Yorkshire Television debate on the state of the cricket before allowing himself to be interviewed on the following night. He is centre-stage at any press conference and he has to feature at any presentation or publicity exercise to do with the county.

Like Mountgarret, he has no cricket background, which means he is often at a distinct disadvantage. I have been in the game long enough to shy away from the suggestion that only former players understand how to run a club — too many of them would be hard pressed to organize a three-table whist drive — but Walsh has not played at even a modest level, nor has he served with any league, so he has no point of genuine contact with the game outside the confines of the Yorkshire club. He is so wrapped up in his own importance, however, that he is totally divorced from the reality of the situation. Had he suffered the agonies of losing and the joy of winning in no more than a scratch evening league match he might appreciate at least some of the problems. Lancashire's Bob Bennett captained their second team and did not make the county grade, but he emerged as a dynamic force within the county as chairman because he has a real feeling for cricket.

Communication is an essential element in the smooth running of any business, yet, as we have seen, Mountgarret is extremely poor in this direction and so is Walsh, despite his reputation as a man of words. True, the chairman can be entertaining and witty as an after-dinner speaker, but he is far too quick to score debating points in committee, seeking to put down his supposed colleagues. It is almost like a parlour-game at times as he digs deep into his Queen's Counsel bag to pull out a big word, leaving the committee to follow his lectures as best they can. This does not help him to establish meaningful relationships, however. It serves merely to intimidate the less confident, though I myself find nothing to be ashamed about in asking him to explain, a tactic which unsettles Walsh because it usually provokes some mirth and consequently pricks his precious dignity.

His lack of consideration has gone so far as to cause great inconvenience to the rest of the committee. Walsh, to my certain knowledge, altered the dates of two management committee meetings and a general committee meeting to suit his social programme. He changed one in order to take his wife to Barbados for their wedding anniversary, which is out of order. The dates for all meetings during a year are fixed well in advance to give all concerned a chance to make their plans and each member of the committee is warned of the days on which his attendance will be required at Headingley. If an individual cannot turn up, that is too bad, but Walsh has made himself a special case. Again he matches the president in pomposity because he believes it so vital to be present. Perhaps he has been afraid that Mountgarret will get up to mischief if he is away and he knows there is no way he could rely on the minutes to give him an accurate impression of what had been said and done.

As a rule Walsh edits the minutes and he is so careful in what is said in the final version that he is not likely to trust the work of another hand. Notes are taken by a shorthand typist and from these Walsh picks and chooses bits to include in the minutes which can be read by any member taking the trouble to approach the secretary. The chairman leans towards the comments that follow the line of his thinking and my contribution to any debate is generally overlooked. At the same time, if the committee agrees on a course of action Walsh will say: 'I'll deal with that, leave it to me.' It is always 'I' and 'me', but with such a big administrative team he should delegate. The aim should be to keep Yorkshire moving forward with everyone playing some part. An example of where delegation would have brought about results is when Vann was pushing hard for a commercial manager and Walsh promised to get some advice from a friend on the pros and cons. Time went by and all enquiries were stonewalled, so nothing happened. Another is when a problem arose at the Hull cricket-ground at the end of the 1989 season and again Walsh took charge with his customary efficiency as we waited and waited, being put off until we all forgot what we were trying to sort out in the first place. With Walsh it is always tomorrow, which never comes. Vann should have been left to produce a draft proposal of his plans and grounds chairman David Drabble should have been asked to deal with Hull, but, no, Walsh has to be the top man. It does not matter to him that because he is busy in his professional life Yorkshire cricket drifts along in the doldrums, unable to make any positive move until he breezes in with a few minutes to spare. Instead of seeking help and using the club's vast secretarial resources, he keeps all the cards close to his chest.

Walsh is consistent if nothing else, so he also insists that only he and the president and the chairman of the various sub-committees are allowed to make public pronouncements. The rest of us are supposed to keep quiet. Well, I can just about accept that, because nothing would be gained if everyone on the committee expressed his personal view on every subject. Sometimes I might not be too happy, but, all right, I understand Walsh's reasoning. The spokesmen do, however, have a responsibility to put each and every case fairly. They enjoy access to the media and to the columns of the *White Rose* magazine, which is distributed among the membership, so it is up to them to mention arguments that have been put forward even if they do not agree with them. That would be the democratic way. A lot depends on the press being supplied with accurate accounts of the various meetings, but sadly this does not happen.

In the circumstances, it is important to remember that Walsh got himself elected to the committee after speaking on my behalf at the special meetings in Harrogate in 1978 and 1984. Twice he earned enthusiastic applause for passionate addresses, during the course of which he used his great ability as an orator metaphorically to pin the old committee to the floor and walk all over it. In that way he helped me a lot, although I did not ask him to campaign for me. I did not know him then and he was approached, I later learned, by Fielden. Having pinned his colours firmly to my mast, he then made his play to establish himself in his own right.

When it became clear in 1984 that the Yorkshire committee would have to resign over the vote of no confidence at Harrogate, Walsh approached Matthew Caswell, a prominent barrister who gave sound advice to the Reform Group, asking if he could stand for election as one of the three Leeds district representatives. What he really needed was a foot in the door and if it was via the Reform Group so be it. He attended a meeting at Caswell's house to meet the other candidates representing the Reform Group, and took full part in the talks which formulated a sort of manifesto.

Having gained election on my coat-tails, Walsh jumped ship as soon as he was elected and I recall clearly the first press conference given by the new regime at which he went to great lengths to stress his independence. With no allegiance to any faction, he made it clear he would remain neutral, which would have been fine if he had made his position clear to people who had voted for him beforehand.

181

The next step was to put himself forward as chairman, contesting the office with Kirk. Although beaten in a couple of battles, he laid long-term plans to win the war, undermining Kirk with a quiet word here and a damaging comment there. Always out to impress with a neat phrase or a telling speech, Walsh acted his part to the full, stressing that he could be useful in his high-ranking social position. He wove a spell which obscured so many realities, savaging Kirk when Headingley lost its place on the permanent Test match rota. In fact, Kirk accepted the inevitable as the Test and County Cricket Board reacted to financial considerations and he did his best to save something from the wreckage of the county's hopes.

Headingley's position as the only permanent Test centre outside London had owed much to Yorkshire's illustrious history and to the forceful personality of Brian Sellers, the distinguished former captain, who represented its interests with great gusto at Lord's. However, it was difficult to justify such preferential treatment, given that Headingley never matched Lord's or the Oval in either attendances or receipts. The other counties made it crystal clear that they were not prepared to let Headingley remain a special case, so Kirk realistically settled for what he could get – two limited-overs internationals in 1990 when Yorkshire's thirty-year run of unbroken Test cricket came to an end. Walsh perpetuated the myth that he himself could have done better, and over the years has been ever ready to recount stories of his successes when he occasionally visits Lord's, although he is extremely careful that no-one in his audience is in a position to contradict him. At every opportunity he continued to attack and belittle Kirk in or out of committee. He transformed normal business into a minefield of argument, giving Kirk no peace until the latter gave up the unequal fight and resigned.

Being no fool, Walsh acknowledges tacitly that he cannot expect to win many arguments about cricket and knows no more than me about making and managing money. But he rarely resists the temptation to portray Geoffrey Boycott in an unfavourable light. A case in point was the famous crisis meeting at Headingley on 10 October 1989. I intend to discuss this gathering in some detail, for these few hours crystallized all that is wrong with the club, but the main issue to which Walsh drew attention was my early departure from that meeting, implying to the press that I had stormed out when I could not get my own way. This bit of nonsense instantly turned into a *cause célèbre* and the headlines announced another Yorkshire row. How much wiser Walsh would have been to deflect any questions about me by telling the press that I was the only person who could account for my action. After all, I had stuck it for three and a half hours, and the treasurer had made his excuses and departed before me. I can, as it happens, remember several meetings before he became chairman at which Walsh arrived late, stayed no more than half an hour, spoke once to catch everybody's eye and then disappeared with his attendance mark safely recorded.

Fielden trod a parallel path to prominence, using his association with me as a stepping-stone from obscurity, and for many years I trusted him like a brother. Without raising my suspicions, Fielden took over completely as my spokesman, encouraging the idea that I followed his advice and that he dictated my actions. It was a massive ego-trip. I sometimes look back and worry about the words he put into my mouth over a long period, wondering how far his activities went towards widening the gulf between me and the club. After all, people at all levels were convinced that anything Fielden said reflected my opinion. There was a particularly damaging period when he remained on friendly terms with me while acting as a bitter enemy, hammering away at the dual role I fulfilled when serving on the committee as a player. Odd bits of news started to drift back to me in late 1984 and eventually I tackled him. He protested that his loyalties were unchanged, but it soon became clear that he was rapidly changing horses to join the cavalry charge hoping to drive me off the committee.

On 1 February 1985 Fielden sent me a strange letter which reflected the confusion in his mind. It read: 'If you pick up a starving dog and make him prosperous, he will not bite you. This is the principal difference between a dog and a man. Written by Mark Twain: *Pudd'nhead Wilson's Calendar*, Chapter 3.' I could only suppose that, because he had helped me a lot and given me a voice when I needed one, Fielden thought I should remain forever in his debt.

One of his earliest victims in his new guise turned out to be Roy Ickringill, who beat the club's cricket chairman and former Yorkshire captain Ronnie Burnet in the 1984 elections to become representative for Harrogate. Ickringill arranged a members' meeting at the local cricket club and I agreed to join him on the platform. Fielden, as public relations chairman, used these occasions to project his image, but Ickringill specifically asked him to stay away from Harrogate so that he could avoid a disruptive debate on my dual role. Ignoring this request, Fielden made a nuisance of himself, upstaging Ickringill and using his greater experience in the cut and thrust of debate to make him look small in front of his own members. I was very angry but realized that if I joined in matters must become worse, so I kept my peace, hoping that things would calm down. I drove home, though, in an angry mood, sickened by the lengths to which Fielden, no doubt spurred on by Stott and Appleyard who were in the audience, would go to get at me.

Anyone who is in the public eye has to be careful about choosing his friends because there are always those looking to use the famous as a prop for their own egos. I have been fortunate in having many good friends, men of real substance like my solicitor Duncan Mutch and Matthew Caswell, a successful barrister. I also trusted Fielden implicitly and

184

through me Caswell did him many favours without wanting payment or anything else in return. Reform Group meetings were held at Caswell's home, with Fielden as the leading figure, and after the members overturned the committee in 1984 Fielden suggested it would be a good idea to nominate Caswell for life membership. 'I don't want anything,' Caswell insisted. Six months later Fielden was to label Caswell as a 'mischief maker'. That was typical. Other former friends he turned against include Tony Vann, secretary of the Reform Group; Peter Briggs, best man at Fielden's wedding and for a long time chairman of the Reform Group; and Mike Helliwell, a keen Barnsley member who fought the committee over a number of issues.

Another friend that Fielden turned against was Duncan Mutch, who took over as Yorkshire's solicitor in 1984 in testing circumstances and served them well. One evening Mrs Fielden telephoned me at home to say he was in very serious trouble. I spoke at once to Mutch, who hurried to Doncaster and sorted things out in a firm, professional way, enabling Fielden to emerge without a stain on his character. Incredibly, within a few weeks Fielden launched a furious, unwarranted attack on Mutch in committee and took a leading hand in having him dismissed by the club.

It definitely does not pay to rely on Fielden, as Kevin Sharp too discovered. The left-handed batsman went through a troubled season in 1989, suffering some freak injuries and struggling to achieve any consistently good form. As a married man, he understandably worried about his future under the shadow of rumours that suggested one senior batsman would be released in September. As it turned out, Jim Love was the one to go, but Sharp, in the meantime, had made tentative approaches about a benefit. Fielden assured him that he would press his case, yet shuffled his feet and said nothing when the matter came up in committee. I thought it very unfair for Sharp to be let down in this manner, so I stepped into the breach with satisfactory results. How, then, can Fielden be relied upon to act as public relations chairman? Is it any wonder that Yorkshire is so divorced from the membership and potential paying customers? The public relations chairman's principal concern should be linking the county with the spectators and sponsors and developing harmony at all levels. Fielden does just the opposite.

Fielden claimed all along that he had backed my cause in 1983 when I was sacked as a player because he believed in the justice of it, yet he rebelled whenever I took independent action. He sounded so very plausible and convincing and as a detective sergeant he always did his homework, so he could never be underestimated. He once said in committee: 'I have known Geoffrey Boycott for many years, through sadness and elation, but now I wish I had never met him.' I could say very much the same about him.

Ninety-nine per cent of the people who take an interest in Yorkshire do so because they simply want to watch the team enjoy a degree of success. It is not much to ask when you look back at all the triumphs, but they have so regularly been disappointed and it is this widespread disappointment that has proved such a fertile breeding-ground for discord. No-one would care what the committee did if Yorkshire were prospering. Close, therefore, has the most important job of all as cricket chairman, for he and his sub-committee colleagues truly shape the destiny of the club. But they are a hapless bunch. Stott, by his own admission, hardly ever sees a ball bowled, Platt makes the effort more regularly but is a weak man when it comes to the crunch. Sharpe and Tony Woodhouse, the one non-player, generally keep quiet. Woodhouse does spend thousands of hours following the fortunes of Yorkshire, yet is reluctant to voice an opinion and spends most of his life uncomfortably on the fence, pathetically trying to please all and sundry. As an official group responsible for maintaining the highest traditions, the cricket committee are a waste of time, and I am convinced that Close is an opinionated square peg in a badly cut round hole. He holds one distinction which, in these days of safety-first national selection policies, may never be equalled, having made his England début aged eighteen years and 149 days. When he walked out against New Zealand at Old Trafford in 1949, Close was the new golden boy, the youngest to represent his country, destined for one of the great careers. Most of that promise remains unfulfilled, however, for he finished with a mere twenty-two England caps, with only eighteen wickets to his name; his batting average was 25·34, and he failed ever to make a Test century.

Nor has he done any better in business, so his mishandling of Yorkshire's affairs fits into a familiar pattern. The trouble is that Close cannot concentrate and when he does turn up at the cricket the members grumble that it is not long before he is either in the bar or in the betting-tent. This lack of mental discipline makes him the proverbial jack of all trades and master of none – a genuine case of wasted ability. The pity is that he never learns. In his own mind only bad luck has prevented him becoming a sporting and commercial giant and, typically for a gambler, he blames his many downfalls on this factor. 'Everyone else played for themselves, but I played for the team,' is a persistent theme. The 1961 Test against Australia at Old Trafford provides the perfect illustration of the extent to which Close is a victim of self-delusion. The contest unfolded along fascinating lines, with England needing 256 for victory in the fourth innings. They reached 150–2 at one stage and held the initiative until Richie Benaud, gaining some turn with his leg-spin out of the rough, bowled Peter May round his legs. Close as a left hander decided that the only way to play the ball, with the bowler's dangerous rough patch outside his off stump, was to sweep everything and he soon holed out to Norman O'Neill at backward square leg as Australia took the honours. The way Close tells the story is that he was unlucky to be out because O'Neill was actually in the wrong position, twenty yards away from where he should have been. Well, for my money I could never accept that Benaud would have a man anywhere but on the spot he wanted him, so I asked Richie about the incident and received a logical explanation. 'Brian was sweeping away,' he told me, 'so at the end of an over I quietly instructed O'Neill to move those twenty yards, emphasizing that I did not want to have to make any signal. The next over from my end, Brian miscued to O'Neill, who made a difficult catch look easy.' Close, therefore, got out not through any ill-fortune but because he did not take the elementary precaution of ensuring that he knew all the field-placings.

It was incredibly careless, with so much at stake. I can honestly say that I checked the field before every ball I ever received in any form of cricket, working on the basis that it is not up to them to tell me where they are standing. Bowlers do lay traps and switch the field between deliveries, the code of conduct universally accepted requiring only that there is no significant movement once the bowler has started his run-up.

Ian Botham recounts the adventures associated with the climax to a Benson and Hedges tie as Close captained Somerset against Surrey at the Oval. The match moved to a nail-biting climax, with Surrey requiring two from the last ball, at which point Close set the field for Alan Jones, who did all he could by pitching into the blockhole around the line of the leg stump. With the batsman slogging, the ball hit the pads and somehow squeezed out wide of point on the thinly populated off side – Close gave chase with third man running round to supplement his effort. As the batsmen raced through for one Close shouted 'Mine, mine.' Dutifully, the third man slowed down, only to see his captain slip and concede two runs to lose the match. Close had lost his footing while wearing crêpe-soled boots on a wet outfield – the height of stupidity. Needless to say, Close immediately gave Jones a fearful dressing-down for bowling the ball in the wrong place.

Actually, Close enjoyed one stroke of tremendous good fortune, in that the Yorkshire team he captained contained so many good players, who matched ability with experience. They could handle his erratic approach without it unsettling them and still rise to the occasion and win. John Barclay, who captained Sussex with a good deal of style, once said to me: 'There are players when you are trying to chase runs and win a game on a declaration who are willing to have a go. They aim a few quick swipes, perhaps hitting a couple of boundaries, and then get out, coming back to say, "I've done my best, skipper. I've sacrificed myself for the team." They haven't helped at all, though. What they have done is to throw away their wicket by abdicating their responsibility and are no more use than an ornament back in the pavilion. It is so much harder to stay in and try to win the game the hard way. If you battle through and fail, you get criticized.' Close adopted that 'over the top' attitude, even at Lord's in 1963, when he did so well against some aggressive West Indian fast bowling. He almost threw away all he had gained by courage and hard work when he walked foolishly down the pitch and got out slogging.

Taking everything into account, the leading characters are not exactly star material, and for this reason the crisis meeting in October 1989 degenerated into a farce. Eric Houseman, the committee-member for Harrogate, summed up the proceedings before they got underway: 'The most we can hope for is to avoid a winter of discontent with a good public relations exercise, but really I do not see what the cricket committee can do.' Close followed up with a lot of excuses, although he did accept that some heads had gone down and that generally the batting was not good enough.

While I sat back and waited for some positive thoughts, the cricket chairman quickly departed into the realms of fantasy, complaining that Keith Boyce had not provided the right type of pitches at Headingley. Close argued that he had wanted more grass taking off and that he could not control the groundsman. That was not even factually correct, for in 1989, after some disagreements the previous year, the owners handed over complete authority for the cricket square to Yorkshire. Close was equally in the wrong when he claimed that the players could not get decent practice strips. If this had been such an important issue, why had he not mentioned it before at any committee meeting? In any case, all he had to do was give Boyce a specific, written instruction and mention it to the Leeds club management, who employ the groundsman. It may be relatively easy for a former England captain to pull the wool over the eyes of some of the committee, but I could pick so many holes in Close's defence of his own position. Nobody knows more about practice than me, and I never had any trouble at Headingley. I made sure that Boyce got two or three days' notice when I intended to have a net and everything was always ready. As I told Close, the fault lay more with the players, who displayed little interest in serious practice. Close sat tight-lipped because he had no answer. All he offered were feeble, half-hearted explanations which cut no ice with anyone who knows a lot about first-class cricket. The situation at Yorkshire puts a lot of responsibility on me as I am the only ex-player outside the cosy little group which runs things, the only person who can challenge them on their own ground and knock them down, one by one, with detailed arguments. So I dismissed Close's claim that the pitches and weather had been against Yorkshire.

I pointed out that 1989 was the best summer in living memory for groundsmen, who had been able to keep pitches as dry as they liked, watering by hand, so Yorkshire could have had the best practice pitches of all time. I further reminded Close and company that it always rains in Yorkshire in March and April, a fact of life with which the club has coped for 127 years, doing quite well at times. The weather pattern is not likely to change much, either.

Close spotlighted the case of Martyn Moxon. 'He did not start until mid-May because of a broken bone in his arm, so he had the best practice conditions and played better than most,' he argued. That did not wash. Even the ordinary committee members appreciate that Moxon, a Test cricketer after all, might just be more skilled than the rest. Being a more accomplished technician, he might also have practised more thoughtfully than his colleagues, many of whom slog the ball around for fifteen minutes and then get bored.

Both Close and Walsh took pains to stress the seriousness of the injuries, but Tony Vann drew attention to Worcestershire's championship-winning side which lost the services of Phil Newport and Graham Dilley, both Test seamers, as well as Ian Botham and Paul Pridgeon, all through injury. They plugged the gaps, with Stuart Lampitt and Steve McEwan emerging from the second team, while Essex had Graham Gooch, Neil Foster and Derek Pringle in the Tests and also coped with their share of injuries to finish second in the championship, after losing 25 points for an unsatisfactory pitch at Southend. Everything Close said carried an air of resignation and he virtually shrugged off the fact that the present generation was 'reluctant to listen and learn' and that it did not possess the 'ability to deal with the moving ball'.

This represented a mental somersault on the part of a man who, as soon as the committee had got me out of the way in 1986, justified my sacking by telling the world that I stifled the development of the 'very talented' young batsmen lining up to take over in the first team. He echoed the same sentiment after the Benson and Hedges Cup Final triumph at Lord's in 1987, trampling all over the committee code of conduct as he proclaimed to the tabloid press: 'We couldn't have done this with Boycott in the team.' Two years later he had to admit that there was a shortage of expertise and a lack of an experienced, quality player to provide stability and give guidance. Belatedly facing up to the realization that most Yorkshire batsmen have gone backwards instead of improving, Close suffered a rush of blood to the head, saying that he could still play better than them one-handed. David Welch of Rotherham lashed into Close for making such a stupid remark. 'That's ridiculous,' he snapped. 'Do you think it would help matters if we told the players how you really feel?' Still thrashing about wildly, Close grumbled that there was no-one in the dressing-room to pass on accumulated knowledge in the way the senior professionals had always done in the past. Well, before Close and his mates sacked me at the end of 1986 I volunteered to undertake that very task, being prepared to bat in the middle-order, or wherever Close dictated. I could have given Yorkshire the benefit of my twenty-five years' experience in top-class cricket all over the world, but Close and the cricket committee were not interested.

In case anybody asks – after I was sacked as captain in 1978 it was made plain by certain members of the committee that my views were not required and that I should 'just bat'.

They clearly did not trust me and Close had said as much in 1986, but in pursuing the youth policy and promising what Walsh called 'golden days' they put their reputations on the line. For three years I had stayed well away from the cricket, leaving them to get on with things and they had failed miserably. Despite all the evidence, Close doggedly persisted with the theory that Yorkshire's poor results were my fault. 'You did not teach them anything when you were captain,' he claimed, yet I pointed out that Arnie Sidebottom and Bairstow, two of my protégés, stood out as the best professionals in the contracted squad.

'So, what about Carrick?' asked Close. He was suggesting that the captain, soon to be removed from office, had failed Yorkshire because I had not taught him properly in the past. 'Well, you thought enough of Carrick to make him captain in 1987 and tell the members what a fine fellow he was,' I answered. Some of the committee struggled not to laugh as Close collapsed like a pricked balloon. All the rest of the Yorkshire side which did so badly in 1989 grew up under other captains and under Illingworth as team manager, so that was another bullet in the foot from the cricket chairman's own gun.

When Close floundered to a halt, the cricket committee tried another tack by asking me for some constructive suggestions. It seemed strange after all that had gone before, but I gave them the benefit of the doubt and invited the committee to take stock of the coaching situation. There is no doubt that the grass-roots are flourishing, not as much as we might like, perhaps, but the Yorkshire schools possess a proud record nationally and the Yorkshire Cricket Association teams usually dominate the under-16 and under-19 age-groups. Many boys reach the stage at which the county take over, and this is where Doug Padgett, the Yorkshire coach, comes into the picture. The position is simple. If, as the committee has suggested for almost twenty years and as junior officials believe, there is talent available, then the coaching must be poor. Otherwise, Yorkshire would not be in such desperate straits. That is not so much opinion as fact.

Padgett has been chief coach for seventeen years, yet Close expected me, not him, to pay the price of the team's failure. It does not add up and I told the committee exactly that. Padgett is a very pleasant, easy-going person, but he is also a weak link. He does not command the respect of all the players. In 1989, after travelling with the first team, he reported back that they did not take any notice of him. Yet the cricket committee cheerfully overlooked his shortcomings. Stott tried to explain that Padgett was hesitant and indecisive because his job had been on the line since 1982. Whose fault is that? Taken at face value, it means that for seven years the cricket committee did not see fit either to give him security or get somebody else. Stott also said he thought Padgett had grown up a lot in the last few months of the 1989 season – an incredible comment on a man of sixty. Finally, Stott said that Padgett's attitude had been shaped by the fact that he was not exactly sure how far his authority extended. Whose fault was that? Was Stott *really* saying that our coach for seventeen years was worried about how far he ought to go?

An incident at Northampton revealed Padgett's limitations, particularly as he was supposed to be there specifically to encourage a more professional attitude. Opening batsman Ashley Metcalfe had been lbw a number of times without playing a shot. He padded up and shouldered arms at Northampton and was despatched yet again lbw. On his return to the pavilion, Padgett, not really ready to believe the evidence of his eyes, asked: 'What on earth happened, then?' Metcalfe, not a bit abashed, replied: 'I thought it would be an outswinger.' Padgett, a pretty good batsman himself, was understandably puzzled. 'How do you mean, you thought it would be an outswinger?' 'I thought by the look on his face he was going to bowl an outswinger,' insisted Metcalfe. Shaking his head in amazement, Padgett asked: 'How does an outswinger look on a bowler's face?' This provoked a good deal of amusement as Metcalfe had meant it to be funny, but he would not have dared to be so flippant with our previous coach, 'Ticker' Mitchell. Nor would he have dared to get out in such a thoughtless way. Mitchell ruled with the proverbial rod of iron and was feared and respected by everyone in the club. If he had to tell anybody twice about anything they had better watch out. Padgett is not tough enough to give those that warrant it a firm kick up the backside, or to motivate others. The lads are on an easy ride and laugh at him, but they would definitely not have laughed at Mitchell if he was in the same room. This is something that the cricket committee does not understand.

Having given my reasons, I proposed that Padgett be moved sideways because I genuinely believe that he has much to offer with the juniors, well away from the first team. I specifically stated that I did not advocate his sacking, as in the past the club had wasted too much time and money trying to sack me. I regarded this as a positive move, but the cricket committee dismissed it as being negative.

Trying another shot in the dark, Close indicated that more money would be needed to produce a better team, at which Sokell raised the pertinent question: 'If you believe the players are not good enough, why pay them more?' At every turn Close ran into further trouble. 'If I had my way I would restrict contracts to one year,' he said, forgetting that he had been happy to award four-year terms to Moxon, Metcalfe, Richard Blakey, Paul Jarvis and Phil Robinson two years earlier. Silence reigned supreme while the committee digested this dazzling piece of inconsistency.

Walsh, the happy optimist in the reflected glory of the 1987 Benson and Hedges Cup celebrations, pessimistically wondered whether too much was now expected of our team and, as the debate went round in meaningless circles, one thing became clear. The cricket committee had no idea how to halt the decline. They rejected any criticism, and nodded approval at the stream of excuses from Close, clinging to office with grim determination. Gratefully they agreed to go away to investigate the merits or otherwise of having a team manager and to define the roles of the captain and coach, something any one of them should have been able to do at the drop of a hat. Absolutely brilliant. We had had the same captain for three years and the same coach for seventeen, so it was a bit late to start finding out what jobs they should be doing!

Stott pushed and prodded at me, asking what I would do. His actions betrayed his inadequacy. I tried to convince the committee that no steps forward could be taken until we had identified the mistakes, but according to the cricket committee none had been made.

There was nothing left to say. I ran out of patience with the muddled thinking and turned my back on it, leaving Headingley bowed down more by sorrow than anger.

11

The way ahead

There is nothing to be gained by beating about the bush – a major clear-out is the only answer for Yorkshire. There has been too much tinkering in the past as endless controversy has filled the dark winter days, creating the illusion that Yorkshire was tackling the problems. Despite the in-depth inquiry, stretching through the second half of 1981 and into 1982, constant turmoil, newspaper polls and trial by television, Yorkshire has stumbled along, with the committee making a few cosmetic changes to paper over the cracks. The personnel and philosophies remain the same, the odd departure heralding the arrival on the scene of a replacement with conservative, conventional views, and I defy anyone to tell me the difference between Close and Walsh in 1989 and Ronnie Burnet and Michael Crawford as cricket chairman and general committee chairman in 1984. Thick-skinned, safely tucked away behind the barrier of self-esteem, the committee rides out the annual storms before basking in the calm waters of summer privilege.

Despite the creation of a fine cricket school at Headingley, which Yorkshire owns, the members remain Yorkshire's most important asset. They can see how bad things are and increasingly they vote with their feet. The high point was 1978, when the membership figure stood at 13,300. That was my last year as captain and since then, despite all the official claims that better, brighter days were just around the corner, the membership has dropped by 4,000. For more than eleven years the warning signals have gone unheeded at Headingley, despite the serious financial implications. The loss adds up to £199,000 a year at 1990 subscription rates, with the treasurer anxiously budgeting for a £9,000 deficit in 1991. There is disillusionment among the membership, not just because the team has performed badly, with the exception of the 1987 Benson and Hedges Cup triumph, but more because they can see no hope, no sign of necessary changes being made. Indeed, many were angered by the committee decision to recommend that members should vote against two resolutions at the 1990 annual meeting. The first advocated reducing the committee to sixteen and the second sought to abolish the cricket committee following the appointment of a manager. These were issues upon which members could well make up their own minds and the committee action was a monstrous act of self-preservation, with Brian Close leading the way as he fought to hold on to his position as cricket chairman. Once more the 'we know best' attitude prevailed.

The cricket committee is particularly guilty of ignoring mistakes, sitting tight as the walls tumble down around its ears. Test selector Phil Sharpe, a disaster as vice-captain under me, persuaded the electors of York to put him on the committee in 1979. He spent the customary probationary year 'learning the ropes' before taking root on the cricket committee for nine of the next ten years. He missed out in 1985, when, like the other ex-players, he refused to serve under chairman Tony Vann. Close and Appleyard exercised power on this influential body for five out of six years, Stott for five out of seven and Platt for two, yet not one of them has ever stood up and said he might just have been wrong on the odd occasion.

The members have been extremely unhappy about the cricket committee for many years, and most of the political upheaval has been brought about by the failure of this body. Dominated by the ex-players, the cricket committee has followed a sorry pattern in repeating errors. At the special meeting in Harrogate in 1978 called to challenge my removal from the captaincy, the cricket committee survived a vote of no confidence by a comparatively small figure. It was not so fortunate in 1984, when a vote of confidence in it after my sacking failed by 3,209 to 3,997. The strength of feeling surprised even my supporters, who successfully brought about my reinstatement as a player. After my sacking in 1986, Close informed the press that there was a place available on his cricket sub-committee, but somehow he never got round to telling me that. In 1989, in accordance with tradition, the various sub-committee chairmen handpicked the men they wanted to work with and Close stuck by his pals. Appleyard, admittedly, did suddenly ask: 'Why don't you come on to the cricket committee, Geoff?' Close said nothing. Not until the first day of the Four Counties' Knockout at the Scarborough Festival in September did Close actually mention the cricket committee and then he waited until he saw me in the luncheon tent.

Glass in hand, he asked: 'Why don't you come on to the cricket committee instead of Appleyard?' I did not take him seriously. He had hardly spoken to me throughout the summer, effectively turned his back on me in March and regularly accused me of ruining the team, yet he wanted to use me to oust a supposed friend of his who had helped him push through the academy at Bradford Park Avenue. It did not make sense and I ignored him. The fact that the story appeared in the *Yorkshire Evening Post* a couple of days later gave the game away. Only two people knew of that brief exchange, and I certainly mentioned it to no-one.

Towards the end of the worst season in the club's history Close was presumably anxious to appease the members, who were making ominous noises. He had not wanted me at the start of the summer, when he persuaded himself that the team might do reasonably well, so his change of heart must have come about in an attempt to win some credibility for the committee through me.

In the circumstances, I do not see how I could achieve anything by being on the cricket committee. I would be outvoted on every single issue and then expected to keep my mouth shut in general committee, bound to silence by the gag of collective responsibility. Loyalty to the other people on the cricket committee would be demanded and they would have me as a prisoner. At least as a general committee member I can stand up and spotlight some of the rubbish that Close tries to pass off as sound cricket sense. This is the only way I have of bringing any sort of pressure to bear on those responsible for so much damage to Yorkshire cricket.

Jim Love stood up as a witness for the prosecution at Northallerton, shortly after being sacked, when Sid Fielden arranged a public relations exercise and ran into a hostile audience. They gave Fielden a rough ride and then in the bar afterwards put the question to Love: 'What's wrong with Yorkshire cricket?' Love said that Carrick was the worst captain he had played under, the cricket chairman was a joke and that the players got too soft an option, with the cricket committee refusing to impose discipline and thus creating the worst dressing-room atmosphere of his career. One more damning indictment of the cricket committee. I would simply disband it as part of a complete clear-out and reshaping of the club management.

I would not, however, replace the cricket committee with a manager. Worcestershire and Essex are two counties to do well without having one. In 1978 I expressed my reservations forcefully when I discovered that Illingworth had been appointed to take over as manager of Yorkshire the following year. My objections, raised before the committee stripped me of the captaincy, may even have counted heavily against me in the final calculations, for I made it crystal clear to Illingworth that I would not be dictated to on the field. The captain must be in charge, as Illingworth was at Leicester, where he indulged in the polite formalities of keeping chief executive Mike Turner informed of any reasonably big decisions. Turner, for his part, stood back and let Illingworth run the show, but Illingworth did not do the same when he arrived at Yorkshire. He imposed his thinking on the captain and his approach led to trouble, as I had expected. I went on the MCC tour to Australia in 1965–6 when Mike Smith as captain was under the control of the manager, Billy Griffith, an experiment that failed and was never tried again. You could not meet two nicer men and they got on well together with no personality clashes, but the manager could not run the cricket from the dressing-room. I noticed when South African Eddie Barlow accepted the managership at Gloucestershire in November 1989 he promptly laid down guide-lines, which indicated his intention to take the pressure off the captain, Tony Wright. If a player has a technical problem, fine, Barlow is there to lend a hand, but he does not intend to interfere with Wright's handling of Gloucestershire during the hours of play. Barlow, in fact, has slipped comfortably into the role of senior coach and adviser before he starts his job, which is exactly what Yorkshire needs.

I would put a forceful, aggressive coach alongside the captain, to form a closely knit partnership, someone like Barry Wood or Peter Willey, who both relish a challenge and don't mince words. Sure, they may offend people, but their directness is the best reason for employing them. Harsh words do have to be used. We talk about 'playing' cricket, but it is a very serious business out in the middle, and there's no room for faint hearts or social graces. Cricketers are not a race apart and, in common with workers in commerce and industry, some of them need reminding sharply of their duties – especially some of the Yorkshire team. Australian wicketkeeper Rodney Marsh told me about his early days in the Test side. He did not exactly impress in the first few games, earning the nickname 'Iron Gloves' as the ball continually bounced out of his grasp and on to the grass. Eventually, Australian captain Ian Chappell enquired, 'Is that ball hot?', sprinkling the question with a choice selection of well known adjectives. 'No, it's fine,' confirmed an anxious Marsh. 'Well in that case start catching it cleanly or we'll soon find someone else who can,' warned Chappell, leaving Marsh with a clear incentive to get his act together. Marsh and Chappell formed a close friendship, but the wicketkeeper never forgot the lesson. The occasional ultimatum would concentrate a few minds in the Yorkshire camp and Wood or Willey could put steel into the dressing-room, making life much easier for the captain. Specialized coaching could be provided as necessary by paying for the best – Illingworth for spinners, Hadlee or Lillee for quick bowlers – experts who could be brought in when available.

The committee may well point to the promotion of Steve Oldham as cricket manager, but it is a tentative step sideways as much as forward, as Steve operates in conjunction with the cricket committee. Oldham had a say in the sacking of Carrick to make way for Moxon with the result that, however you look at it, the new captain owes his position in part to the manager. Moxon's independence is threatened, which is wrong, just as it was when Hampshire and Old operated in the shadow of Illingworth's patronage. The committee, cut down to a more reasonable size, should appoint the captain and the coaching staff, and judge them on results. Definitely Doug Padgett is not the man to be at the forefront of the action.

I would dispense with second team captain Neil Hartley as well. Appointed by Close, he is not my idea of the type who should help youngsters bridge the enormous gulf between the second eleven and first-team cricket.

Hartley did nothing as a player to earn a cap and is a poor technician with little to contribute beyond an agility in the field, which is fine when it is a bonus allied to other skills but is not enough on its own. A second-team captain with a better pedigree and another down-to-earth coach would do much to boost the county's prospects as part of a comprehensive package. The first team is the flagship of Yorkshire cricket, sailing along smoothly so long as the engine-room is running efficiently. Steps should be taken, therefore, to oil the machinery below decks, where there is scope for Padgett to be usefully employed at junior level.

The standard in the leagues has dropped alarmingly over the years and it is symptomatic of the way things are going that two major clubs, Leeds and Wakefield, have withdrawn from the Yorkshire League because of a shortage of players, something that would have been unthinkable once upon a happier time. Fewer schools fit cricket into the curriculum and there are now so many different sporting bodies trying to capture the imagination of boys of above-average ability. Big cities such as Leeds employ various development officers pushing the attractions of swimming, athletics, soccer, Rugby League and Rugby Union, so cricket has to compete in the market-place. Additionally, tennis and golf, no longer the preserve of the wealthy, appeal to many. To make sure cricket does not miss out, I would put Padgett into the schools and the leagues, where he could raise the standards of the coaching and stimulate interest in cricket. It is a difficult game to coach unless you really know what you are doing. Soccer is much easier. All a teacher has to do is mark out the goals, throw down the ball and say, 'get on with it'. A lad playing soccer can run about for an hour, have three or four kicks at the ball and still feel he has had a good game because he is out of breath and tired. It's different for a boy standing around in the field for a couple of hours and then lasting no more than a handful of deliveries when it comes to his turn to bat. He thinks cricket is a funny old game and goes on to something else, like golf, where the worse you are the more hits you get. Yorkshire must appoint a coach to go round the schools and the leagues and I would like to see our players getting more involved, particularly as most can no longer afford to go to South Africa in the winter for fear of being banned from Test cricket.

A few years ago I set up coaching courses for both Kevin Sharp and Arnie Sidebottom in Wakefield, Barnsley and Pontefract, using sports centres, which can be booked well in advance. I rang round a few friends and acquaintances who had children aching to be coached and the scheme snowballed. All Sharp and Sidebottom have to do to keep it rolling is get on the telephone in September each year, and they can earn useful money while developing youngsters' interest in cricket. Yorkshire could build on this comparatively small beginning by covering every part of the county to cut down travel and make it convenient for the youngsters and their parents, who have to provide the transport. Once the word got round that a Yorkshire player was coaching, the numbers would quickly grow. The game in Yorkshire is going downhill fast and the first requirement is to apply the brakes. Proper coaching must also be provided at the cricket academy, which is a good idea so far as it goes. Appleyard and Fielden are selling the academy as the answer to everything. It isn't.

The boys who went on to the contracted staff from the academy in 1989, Darren Gough, Matthew Doidge, Paul Grayshon and Jeremy Batty, had already been coached by Padgett and Oldham for at least four years before the academy started, so these four were merely continuing their progress. Fielden devoted a lot of his considerable energy to going round telling all and sundry that the academy would be producing a stream of Test cricketers within a few years, which is nonsense.

Fitness is another source of concern for Yorkshire, with so many key bowlers breaking down season after season. Other counties also suffer and some of the training schedules do as much harm as good. There is a wide variety of programmes, some of which include weird contortions, but the Truemans and Alec Bedsers of the world got through a lot of overs year after year and stayed sound. They gradually built up to peak condition by bowling in the nets. I never indulged in the more vigorous forms of exercise, although I made sure that I looked after myself.

All these things are important if Yorkshire is to halt the sad decline, but the key to a revival on the field is appointing the right captain. The trouble is that the county does not have a good candidate, as is all too clear from recent history. They sacked me in 1978 because, according to the committee, I was not getting the best out of the 'very good' players in the side. Yorkshire finished fourth in the Championship that year – we had been second in 1975 – and has not come anywhere near such a high placing since. In eight out of eleven seasons it figured among the double-figure also-rans and captains have come and gone – John Hampshire (1979–80), Chris Old (1981–2), Illingworth (1982–3), David Bairstow (1984–6), Phil Carrick (1987–9) and now Martyn Moxon.

That list says two things to me – the committee does not know what it is doing and the county is producing immature players with no grasp of what is needed to win the championship. No-one on the contracted staff has experienced the pressures and pleasures of capturing the title. I can recall so clearly the excitement of chasing that top spot as the tension grew. Word might come through that Kent or one of our other rivals had won while we still needed four or five wickets with time running out. Trueman would find another yard of pace and Illingworth would spin his finger raw as we worked and tried every trick in the book. There was never a moment when Yorkshire could relax, but throughout the 1980s the players have become soft and complacent, as Love confirmed. Fewer juniors are coming through to push for selection, so anyone who can bat reasonably well and bowl a bit is virtually guaranteed a place, for up to twelve years. It is not the same for spinners and wicketkeepers. At most, a side has room for only two slow bowlers, one right- and one left-arm, and one wicketkeeper, so an element of luck is involved, to be the first to these postings. Yorkshire did not want to lose Steve Rhodes to Worcestershire in 1985 but he departed because Bairstow, as senior wicketkeeper, was holding him back. There are, though, five or six batting places at any one time, with no lengthy queue to fill them. A few years ago there would have been fifteen or so batsmen with the necessary ability and before that probably twenty-five, and many old players will tell you that they disguised injuries and shrugged off pain because they dare not give someone in the second team the opportunity to challenge for their place. Now it is too easy to hold a place in the team, particularly with the doors barred to outsiders.

The lack of spirit and tactical awareness forced Illingworth out of retirement at fifty to take over the captaincy as well as being manager, in a brave but vain attempt to instil some old-fashioned character into the team.

One incident at the Oval back in July 1975 illustrates exactly what is missing. I left Surrey a target of 266 and for most of the last afternoon they held the initiative on a pitch slightly favouring the spinners. To contain them, I took off Carrick, who did not spin the ball as much as Geoff Cope, and called on Old. He got the wickets which shifted the balance of power, so, with Surrey still around fifty short, I went back to Carrick. 'You're not going to bowl me again are you?' he asked, obviously worried that he might lose the game. 'Of course I am,' I replied. 'How else do you think we're going to win? They'll just put up the shutters if Old continues.' Carrick duly picked up a couple of wickets as Surrey battled against the clock, finally bowling Pat Pocock, and Yorkshire won by 35 runs to climb to the top of the table for the first time in several years. Carrick, buoyed by the success which came as such a surprise to him, regarded me as something of a magician, conjuring up a victory out of nothing, yet all I had done was to apply basic Yorkshire principles. Close used Don Wilson in exactly the same way and it did not take an excess of brain-power to guess that Carrick would be the bowler the Surrey tail-enders fancied, the one against whom they might take a risk. Tightening the screw and then loosening it a thread was, I am sure, standard practice throughout all those glorious seasons when Yorkshire operated on 'automatic pilot'. Each individual understood his own role and how he fitted into the collective pattern, so the amateur captain did little more than ensure that the rigid framework of discipline was not forgotten.

When I first entered the Yorkshire dressing-room, I stood in awe of the famous figures surrounding me, and I was no different from thousands of other young hopefuls. Kids like me grew up with one ambition – to play for Yorkshire – because the great personalities had captured our imagination. Games in the street or on any rough patch of grass involved pretending that we were the stars, and every boy wanted to be Len Hutton.

Those days have gone. Representing Yorkshire has become just another job and an easy one at that. To appreciate the situation, consider the way Martyn Moxon and Ashley Metcalfe play. They are Yorkshire's regular opening pair, the latest in a distinguished line. Moxon has played for England and Metcalfe is mentioned regularly as being on the fringe of selection. Both, however, are content with second best and do not bother to seek improvement. Moxon has been clearly exposed at Test level, for when he plays forward to a good length ball that is not quite there he pushes the left knee forward and then pulls it back, leaving a gap about a foot and a half wide. New Zealand's Richard Hadlee, for one, is too good a seam bowler not to spot that, so he nips one back and bowls him, and other leading pacemen have spotted the weakness too. Moxon should never be bowled like that. It is a technical fault which has exposed him time and time again at the highest level, and should have been ironed out by now, but I don't see him doing anything about it. If he sorted it out he would have his leg in the way and at worst run the risk of a possible lbw.

With Metcalfe it is more a matter of how he feels, how he wakes up in the morning. I like him as a person and admire his talent but, speaking as a professional, I despair at his cavalier approach. He shuffles around the crease and plays across the line. On occasions he simply throws the bat at the ball, revealing a lack of discipline that is amazing when he is so keen to play for England. Metcalfe turned his back on a happy and rewarding winter in South Africa to remain eligible, yet he had never taken the trouble to ask me for any advice. Indeed, until the end of the 1989 season the only Yorkshire batsman to ask for help is Richard Blakey, who approached me at Sheffield in 1988 when he could not seem to get a run, and I promptly fixed him up. Fortunately, I was familiar with his game, so I was able to tell him: 'I guarantee you'll get runs.' This shook him, because he had hit such a terrible patch, but I put it to him straight. 'Look, you have to believe in the man you are asking for guidance. It's not for me to tell you I'm good, you have to be convinced in your own mind. We'll get nowhere if you've come to me because you've been sent. I know I can get you right in five innings and if you have faith in me that is exactly what I'll do.' Not only that, I added that if he trusted me and listened to exactly what I said he would play for England, and I do not make silly predictions. I was confident because I had seen what he was doing wrong. Blakey took notice and picked up at once, going on to score steadily in 1989. I watched him occasionally and was not surprised when at the end of the season he telephoned me to ask for another meeting. We got together at Wortley Golf Club one Sunday morning, where he hesitated before putting into words exactly what was worrying him. 'I'm playing reasonably well,' he said, and I finished the sentence for him: 'but not going on to make big hundreds.' 'That's exactly right,' he confirmed. We talked about why he continually got out caught behind and I told him what not to do, what to practise in Zimbabwe in the winter and about altering the balance of his body, very technical stuff which matters only at the highest level. While I was with England in the West Indies I was pleased to hear of Blakey's success on the Zimbabwean tour, particularly when he made 221 in the 'Test' in Bulaweyo, the big score showing that he had the mental ability to play a really long innings.

Blakey's concern was that he felt his batting was standing still rather than going forward to bigger and better things, so he did something about it, but most players are happy to jog along. They have got themselves into a frame of mind in which they accept that they are no-hopers in the championship, so they step up a gear only in the one-day competitions. There is a bit of luck involved in the Benson and Hedges Cup and the NatWest Trophy and on a good day any county can win through. I think that is a very sorry state of affairs indeed. I could make Metcalfe a much better batsman in a few months, but he is not interested. He is determined to play his own way – standing with his bat in the air and aiming across the line – and that is that. How can he hope to establish himself in the England line-up? At his age I had a thousand questions for Trueman and Illingworth. Why did they think I had got out, why had I played and missed, what did they think of a particular incident as bowlers?

Now the players treat county cricket like a Saturday afternoon game. They turn up, have a good time and drift off to the pub or the disco in the evening. They don't want to talk about work.

This, of course, is the lifestyle of the ordinary cricketer, the one doing well enough to get by on the circuit, the one who will never make a good captain. Logically, then,

Yorkshire should look elsewhere and that means going outside the county to recruit a world-class overseas player, a full-time professional like Richard Hadlee or Clive Rice or Malcolm Marshall – someone totally committed. I appreciate that such a move cannot be undertaken lightly and I have given the matter very careful thought. In the first place, the proud boast that Yorkshire uses only players born within the county is a myth, and that cannot be stressed too strongly. I'm all for tradition but not one based on falsehood. The trouble is that too few people are aware of the truth. They still believe the myth, which is part of the county's folklore, growing all the time with the telling. I grew up firmly convinced that only those born within the Broad Acres had ever played for the club, only to learn later that this was far from being the case. Twenty-nine 'outsiders' have figured in Yorkshire teams down the years. It is not a question of the odd one somehow slipping through the screening process: even Lord Hawke, the great father-figure of Yorkshire cricket, was a 'foreigner', born in Lincolnshire. The idea of breaking with supposed 'tradition' is not new, for I drew attention to the fact that Yorkshire competed with one hand tied behind its back when I was captain, while in 1989 Carrick, the players and the cricket committee all came to the conclusion that the county at present does not possess the ability to win the championship.

Fred Trueman speaks for many when he says: 'The day Yorkshire engages an overseas player I will drive to Headingley and hand in my membership.' That is all right by me. He is an honorary member anyway and does not pay a subscription as I do, but more important, he is adopting an out-of-date stance. His career stretched across a period when Yorkshire was a great power in the land and when there were not many imported stars strengthening other counties. Although he did subsequently sit on the commit-tee, his contact with the club became too loose to keep him in touch, so he lives in a world that no longer exists.

Appleyard is another former Test star who agrees with Trueman, but Yorkshire cannot remain wallowing in the quicksand of failure to please those who think it is still 1950 or 1960. Nottingham Forest manager Brian Clough is a good friend of mine and he put things neatly into perspective when deep in discussions about Manchester United. The prospect of tackling the most prestigious job in soccer appealed strongly. 'I am happy to crawl up the motorway on hands and knees to get to Old Trafford,' he wrote, adding a telling postscript: 'If I do take over, my first task will be to take the staff on a conducted tour of the trophy room. I will let them see the silverware and then make sure the door is locked and bolted until we have something to put in on our own account.' This angered people who thought Clough was being disrespectful to Sir Matt Busby, manager of United during their great triumphs, but nothing could have been further from the truth. He was, rather, putting Busby on a pedestal, while demonstrating that each group of players has to earn its own rewards.

Yorkshire's members, drawing comfort from the record books, have of course voted heavily against any move to recruit overseas talent and I do not agree with Carrick's suggestion that the club should ignore their clearly expressed wishes. I believe, however, that Yorkshire's desperate situation justifies re-opening the debate. After all, around half the members did not respond when the county twice organized a referendum, so in theory they are open to persuasion. There is also a growing awareness of the difficulties which lie ahead. There isn't another Trueman or another Boycott waiting in the wings and one or two of the diehards are reluctantly reviewing the situation. My Wakefield members know where I stand, but a couple of years ago at a district meeting only a few hands went up to support me on this issue. But by the 1989 meeting thirty per cent indicated their willingness to go down that particular road, so some minds are open and receptive to sensible argument. 'What if we get a poor overseas player?' ask the doubters, but that is a matter of judgement and I am convinced we could find the right man to raise the standards in the Yorkshire dressing-room, to make the players concentrate and give 100 per cent all the time. At the moment they do not know how to go about winning a championship match, being carried along by the tide of events instead of influencing the flow. They have few ideas and one of the most popular tactics involves 'seeing how things go'. The Yorkshire sides that won the championship were always working to a plan, forever talking about the game and making things happen. As soon as one match finished thoughts turned to the next fixture, to the likely composition of the opposing team and the probable conditions. There is no-one left in the team to give the essential lead, so logically the county should recruit an outsider.

I would arrange meetings throughout the county and hold discussions to put the facts truthfully before the members, telling them firmly but honestly that this is the best way and explaining why. We are pathetically short of leadership, which only a very special person can provide. This is where the committee was wrong over the captaincy. Moxon is a very nice chap, but he does not know any more about the game than three or four others in the team.

It would have been far more sensible to give Oldham the captaincy on a short-term basis while conducting a worldwide search for a Barlow or a Rice to take over on a more permanent basis. Being stronger and having studied the game more deeply than Moxon, Oldham would, with the backing of a tough, battle-hardened coach, have been better equipped to mount a holding operation and get Yorkshire playing the right sort of cricket. It is not that Yorkshire has bad players; they have been playing badly with flashes of promise, which proves that they *are* capable of doing much better, given greater discipline and a more demanding environment. Perhaps Oldham could have groomed Moxon and eased him into a position of greater authority just in case Yorkshire's head-hunting expedition ran into difficulties.

Above all else, the priority ought to be the production of a blueprint for the next ten years or, possibly, longer, covering every aspect from the presidency down to the smallest detail of junior development. With the club sinking deeper and deeper, chairman Brian Walsh appears at last to share this view, going on record to say publicly that he favours a complete investigation into the administrative structure by an independent firm of specialists. For once he is on the right lines, although it is a pity he did not speak up in committee and instigate discussion, because some of us could have saved the club a lot of money. Specialists are expensive and our experience on the inside enables us to cut through the dead-wood of clumsy management to get at the root of our difficulties. For example, it is obvious that Yorkshire will never flourish in the midst of so much confusion of purpose.

The system under which twenty-three men represent seventeen districts should be recognized as an anachronism, which served its purpose and worked well enough in the old days when few had cars and even fewer telephones. The only way that a member in, say, Scarborough or Sheffield could discover if anything of interest was happening was to contact his area representative, while if he had a complaint the means existed for it to be relayed to headquarters via his representative, even if it did take weeks or months for a matter to be resolved. This is no longer the case and the committee is unwieldy with divided loyalties. The size of the membership in Bradford and Sheffield no longer justifies these two cities having three men each on the ruling body. I cannot help feeling that Close and Appleyard pushed so hard for the cricket academy to be set up at Bradford Park Avenue because they wanted to please the Bradford members, who vote for them every three years.

A number of schemes have been floated to streamline the committee with various proposals for sixteen or twelve committee-men, but none of these goes far enough. I envisage a maximum of six, elected by all the members at the annual meeting and retiring by rotation. Free from any local pressures, they could serve as the guardians of the club's best interests, answerable to all the members and there to oversee the activities of a chief executive and his staff. This chief executive, like the managing director of a company, would be in charge of the day-to-day business with the authority to hire and fire and make far-reaching decisions in the way Turner does at Leicester, reporting to the committee once a month.

The new chairman could have a significant background role, with the president continuing very much as a figurehead, the role in which Sir Leonard Hutton sees himself. He is a very distinguished figure, far removed from any politics and will, I am sure, restore dignity and stature to the office. I have the greatest admiration for Sir Leonard and it is one of my deep regrets that I did not see him play. I went to Bradford twice, but it rained both times and that was that. Unquestionably, however, he relates to the Yorkshire public in a way Mountgarret never could, commanding popularity and affection for his outstanding contribution to the game.

There are two ways in which the office of chief executive might be filled and, once established, the new committee could explore the possibilities. There may well be a volunteer wealthy enough not to have to work or able to attend to his business when it suits him, sufficiently interested to take over the running of Yorkshire in the way that the late Sir Gubby Allen organized things at Lord's. He would genuinely be a modern-day Lord Hawke, but if that is not possible then Yorkshire must provide a healthy salary to attract a fully qualified person from the world of commerce. Under him I would have an administrative secretary. Alongside him, a commercial manager could improve the overall financial position by marketing the club and making better use of the players. The name of the two games are cricket and making money, and there are so many advantages to be gained from linking more closely with the Leeds club at Headingley. I would definitely have found the means to take up their offer concerning the ground and I am convinced that in the long term Yorkshire will find it expedient to work more closely with them in all sorts of ways, possibly sharing offices to save money. Neither party can afford the loss of the Test match, which in 1989 brought in over £300,000, so the two prominent sporting bodies have a crucial common interest which it is foolish to ignore.

The whole question of grounds merits careful investigation, for the Yorkshire public endures primitive conditions and Headingley is the least comfortable of the Test centres. Yorkshire's policy of playing matches in Leeds, Harrogate, Hull, Sheffield, Middlesbrough and Scarborough to satisfy parochial pressure has left a legacy of neglect and decay which stands as a shameful testament to indifference and selfishness. There is no cover, so an umbrella is essential equipment for the spectator, catering is limited and very expensive, and the toilets are an affront to human dignity, particularly so far as the ladies are concerned. This, then, is an area in which Yorkshire would profit from having a small committee free from conflicting local demands and able to shape policy to suit the majority.

I am certain, as the Wakefield representative with no axe to grind, that Yorkshire should concentrate on three grounds – Leeds, Scarborough and Sheffield. Yes, I can hear the howls of protest from Bradford, Harrogate, Middlesbrough and Hull, but I cannot accept their claims. With vested interest ruling the roost, Yorkshire is not only spreading first-class matches over too many grounds, Yorkshire is also paying rental to these grounds for the privilege, which is ludicrous. The figures at Scarborough are £1,000 for a Sunday League match and £2,000 for a championship game. There is a slight drop at Sheffield and Middlesbrough where the respective figures are £725 and £1,450; the same costs apply to Hull and Harrogate. Over in Lancashire they do the opposite and demand a fee to take a fixture away from Old Trafford. Yorkshire should guarantee in writing that for the next ten or fifteen years they will allocate games to Leeds, as the centre for the West Riding, Scarborough, because North Marine Road is popular with holiday makers and members enjoy the occasional day at the seaside, and Sheffield, with its large catchment area. Such a commitment would encourage the ground authorities to improve the facilities and erect temporary stands and boxes, safe in the knowledge that they could rely on a return from the investment.

The commercial manager could then follow up by persuading local sponsors to play their part in a concerted effort to promote county cricket in their area. The Harrogate Festival, which is invariably oversubscribed, is proof of the potential. I make no apology for repeating that Yorkshire members and the spectators who pay at the turnstile get nothing for their money beyond the right to watch the matches. The rows of empty seats are a growing sign of dissatisfaction, and facilities will have to improve. It is possible to upgrade Scarborough and Sheffield on a more modest scale to make the membership feel they are part of the family instead of unwelcome intruders, and a leaf could profitably be taken out of Surrey's book, for it has done wonders with temporary structures at the Oval.

Headingley must improve, and needs a huge injection of capital to maintain its Test match status. As the Test and County Cricket Board chases bigger profits, Test match fixtures are going to be staged at venues which can cater in the grand manner. Leeds Cricket, Football and Athletic Club has produced some architect's drawings aimed at making the joint football and cricket stand more comfortable. They deserve credit for their enterprise. It should be remembered that Headingley is an institution that does not belong to me, the chairman of Leeds or the president of Yorkshire. It is part of the heritage of Yorkshire cricket. The deeds of ownership are incidental, because thousands of enthusiasts in Yorkshire regard the ground as being something special to them. Over the next twenty or thirty years we need to build an eye-catching complex with covered seating for forty thousand spectators, and all the essential ancillary services, including sponsors' boxes, restaurants and toilets. Nothing can be done in a hurry, but the steps could be taken one at a time. I used to go to Sydney when the famous hill stood out as an oasis of grass, but this has long gone under the bulldozer, being replaced by well-appointed stands which enable the authorities to seat over fifty thousand in comparative luxury. Yorkshire and Leeds must follow this path, too.

Creating the right image through the media is vital. Yorkshire's refusal to provide a steady stream of reliable information has left it to the likes of BBC broadcaster Don Mosey to set themselves up as authoritative voices on the club's affairs. Like Trueman, he is twenty years out of date and hardly ever comes to watch the team play, relying on opinions at second, third and fourth hand, but lack of first-hand experience has never stopped him launching forth. Unhappily, Mosey is not the only journalist to make uninformed comments, so Yorkshire should indulge in more open government to prevent rumour spreading. Admittedly there are issues the committee would need to keep confidential, but these have a habit of cropping up in the newspaper columns anyway.

In the final analysis, it all depends on how much people care about Yorkshire cricket. I care enough to cut the committee drastically and put my own place at risk and I care enough to rip away the camouflage draped over inefficiency and selfishness. I gain nothing from being Wakefield representative, not money, not prestige, but I involve myself in order to put something back into the club.

I don't care about being popular and the bottom line is that I want to restore Yorkshire's once-proud standing. Brian Sellers, as cricket chairman, used to tell the players: 'Enjoy yourselves and win.' Yorkshire doesn't win all that often these days and I am afraid there is precious little enjoyment. Things must not be allowed to drift any longer.

APPENDIX:

Yorkshire's 'foreigners'

in order of appearance

Player	Début	Professional (P)/ Amateur (A)	Matches
J. Hall	1863	P	1*
T. Darnton	1864	P	13
A. J. A. Wilkinson	1865	A	5
W. Smith	1865	P	11
H. W. Verelst	1868	A	3
W. Law	1871	A	4
C. M. Sharpe	1875	A	1
H. M. Sims	1875	A	5
C. W. Landon	1878	A	9
H. E. Rhodes	1878	A	10
M. Burrows	1880	P	6
C. J. Gifkins	1880	A	2
W. Sugg	1881	P	1
Hon. M. B. (later Lord) Hawke	1881	A	510
F. H. Sugg	1883	P	8

*Also played for the county before the club was formed.

J. W. Parton	1889	P	1
W. F. Whitwell	1890	A	10
T. W. Foster	1894	P	14
F. W. Milligan	1894	A	81
T. Tait	1898	P	2
C. H. Parkin	1906	P	1
E. J. R. Radcliffe	1906	A	64
E. Loxley–Firth	1912	A	2
W. E. Blackburn	1919	A	10
R. C. Chichester–Constable	1919	A	1
R. T. Stanyforth	1928	A	3
K. A. Lister–Kaye	1928	A	2
W. E. Harbord	1929	A	16
W. G. Keighley	1947	A	35

Biographical details

W. E. Blackburn   Born at Clitheroe, Lancashire, on 24 November 1888, died 3 June 1941. Was regarded as a very good fast-bowling prospect but did not have the physique to sustain a career in first-class cricket and gave way to Emmott Robinson. Played in 1919 and 1920.

M. Burrows   Born at Chesterfield, Derbyshire, on 8 August 1855, died 29 May 1893. Played in six matches in 1880 without making any real impression. Appeared for Derbyshire once in 1884.

R. C. Chichester-Constable   Born at Wycombe, Buckinghamshire, on 21 December 1890, died 26 May 1963. Played only once for Yorkshire, in 1919. Captained Second XI 1926–38. Served on the county committee.

T. Darnton   Born at Stockton-on-Tees, Durham, on 12 February 1836, died 25 October 1874. A sound batsman and steady bowler of medium pace, his best match figures were 14 and 81 not out and 3–63 against the All England XI at Sheffield in 1865. (In the second innings of this match he went in at the fall of the first wicket and so did not carry his bat through the completed innings as is generally thought.) Played 1864–8.

T. W. Foster Born at Birkdale, Lancashire, on 12 November 1871, died 31 January 1947. A fast-medium right-arm bowler, Foster burst upon the first-class cricket scene in 1894, taking 10 wickets in a match three times in his first four games, but thereafter fell away to take only 11 wickets in his last six matches of the season. Played only once more – in 1895.

G. J. Gifkins Born at Thames Ditton, Surrey, on 19 February 1856, date of death unknown. Played only two matches, in 1880, one of them being against Surrey at the Oval when he made his top score of 23.

J. Hall Born at Nottingham, on 11 November 1815, died 17 April 1888. Associated with Yorkshire cricket for many years in the Bradford area, his only first-class match for Yorkshire was in 1863, against his native Nottinghamshire at Nottingham.

W. E. Harbord Born at Oakham, Rutland, on 15 December 1908. Of the twenty-nine 'foreigners' only he and W. G. Keighley are still alive. Played for Yorkshire sixteen times 1929–35. Played for Oxford University in 1930 (no Blue), then became a member of county committee and eventually vice-president, until he resigned in 1984.

Hon. M. B. (later Lord) Hawke Born at Willingham, Lincolnshire, on 16 August 1860, died 10 October 1938. His career as player and administrator is well documented and, indeed, enshrined in the history of Yorkshire cricket. He did much to improve conditions for professional cricketers, introducing talent-money, winter pay and helping to ensure that the benefit proceeds were not squandered. Appointed captain to succeed Tom Emmett in 1883. He played in only one match in 1885, versus M.C.C. at Scarborough; when asked why he had not played in more matches, he said, 'perhaps they thought I wasn't good enough'. Played 1881–1911.

W. G. Keighley   Born at Nice, France, on 10 January 1925, he is one of only two of the twenty-nine Yorkshire 'foreigners' still living. An Oxford Blue in 1947 and 1948, he scored 99 against Cambridge in the 1947 match. He was a stylish opening batsman who, in his second match for the county, made 51 in a first-wicket partnership of 169 with Len Hutton against the South Africans at Sheffield in 1947. Was captain of Yorkshire Second XI in 1949 and 1950. Played 1947–1951. Now living in Australia.

C. W. Landon   Born at Bromley, Kent, on 30 May 1850, died 5 March 1903. Played six matches for Lancashire before appearing in nine matches for Yorkshire between 1878 and 1882, five of the nine being against the Australians, I Zingari and MCC.

W. Law   Born at Rochdale, Lancashire, on 9 April 1851, died 20 December 1892. A brilliant fielder and hard-hitting batsman, he appeared for the Gentlemen against the Players at Lord's in 1873 and was captain of Oxford University in 1874. Did little in his four matches for Yorkshire, spread over three seasons in 1871–3. He founded the Harrow Mission in Notting Hill and later became Vicar of Rotherham.

K. A. Lister–Kaye (later Sir Kenelm)   Born at Kensington, London, on 27 March 1892, died 28 February 1955. Played only two matches for Yorkshire, in 1928. Played for Oxford University in 1912 (no Blue).

E. Loxley–Firth   Born at Hope, Derbyshire, on 7 March 1886, died 8 January 1949. His only games for the county were against Cambridge University and the Australians in 1912.

F. W. Milligan   Born at Aldershot, Hampshire, on 19 March 1870, died 31 March 1900. After Lord Hawke, Milligan made the greatest contribution to Yorkshire cricket of all the twenty-nine 'foreigners'. A dashing lower-order batsman, a penetrative fast bowler and a superb fielder, he captained the side on a few occasions when Lord Hawke was absent. He was killed in the Boer War during the relief of Mafeking.

C. H. Parkin   Born at Eaglescliffe, Durham, on 18 February 1886, died 15 June 1943. Parkin played only once for Yorkshire, in 1906, before it was revealed that he was born just twenty yards outside the county boundary. Later became one of Lancashire's great bowlers and made ten Test match appearances for England.

J. W. Parton   Born at Wellington, Shropshire, on 31 January 1863, died 30 January 1906. Played only one match for Yorkshire, in 1889. Also played for his native Shropshire.

E. J. R. (later Sir Everard) Radcliffe   Born at Tiverton, Devon, on 27 January 1884, died 23 November 1969. Appointed to succeed Lord Hawke as captain in 1911, he had led the side on many occasions in his Lordship's absence during the two previous seasons. As the 1912 *Wisden* remarked: 'He stood in a very delicate position as whenever he played a better cricketer had to be left out of the team.'

H. E. Rhodes   Born at Hennerton, Berkshire, on 11 January 1852, died 1 September 1889. All of Rhodes's cricket for Yorkshire was played at the Scarborough Festival against MCC and I Zingari. He was a Cambridge rowing Blue. Played 1878–83.

C. M. Sharpe   Born at Codicote, Hertfordshire, on 6 September 1851, died 25 June 1935. A Cambridge Blue with an impressive record. In 1875 he took 66 wickets for the University at an average of 12·84 in six matches, including 11–155 in the match against Oxford. A slow round-arm bowler, Sharpe played only one match for Yorkshire – in

223

1875 – but without success. He was a soccer Blue and later became Vicar of Elsecar, near Barnsley.

Rev. H. M. Sims Born at Tavistock, Devon, on 15 March 1853, died 5 October 1885. Only two of his five matches for Yorkshire were against county opposition, the others being against MCC and I Zingari at Scarborough. Played 1875–7. A Cambridge Blue, contemporary with C. M. Sharpe, he later became Vicar of Hunslet, Leeds.

W. Smith Born at Darlington, Durham, on 1 November 1839, date of death unknown. Made eleven spasmodic appearances over 10 years between 1865 and 1874, but never reproduced his form against Lancashire in 1867 when he made 60 at Manchester and then scored 90 at Middlesbrough.

R. T. Stanyforth Born at Chelsea, London, on 30 May 1892, died 21 February 1964. Played most of his cricket for Army teams and took over the captaincy of the MCC team to South Africa in 1927–8, where he played in four Tests. He played his three matches for Yorkshire in 1928 as a replacement wicketkeeper to Arthur Wood.

F. H. Sugg Born at Ilkeston, Derbyshire, on 11 January 1862, died 30 May 1933. His performances in his eight matches for Yorkshire in 1883 gave no clue to his real potential. After a short stay at Derbyshire he went to Lancashire where, in 13 seasons, he scored almost 10,000 runs and made fifteen centuries.

W. Sugg Born at Ilkeston, Derbyshire, on 21 May 1860, died 23 May 1933. Elder brother of F.H., he made only one appearance for Yorkshire before joining Derbyshire.

T. Tait Born at Langley Moor, Durham, on 7 October 1872, died 6 September 1954. Played only two matches for Yorkshire – one in 1898 and one in 1899.

H. W. Verelst Born at Claughton, Cheshire, on 2 July 1846, died 5 February 1918. An outstanding schoolboy cricketer at Rugby, he played only three matches for Yorkshire in 1868 and 1869 – all at Sheffield.

W. F. Whitwell   Born at Stockton-on-Tees, Durham, on 12 December 1867, died 12 April 1942. In his only season for the county, 1890, he returned some useful bowling performances without threatening to dominate. A fast bowler, his best match was against Lancashire at Manchester when he took 4–24 and 4–59.

A. J. A. Wilkinson   Born at Mount Oswald, Durham, on 28 May 1835, died 11 December 1905. Played for both Yorkshire and Middlesex in four seasons from 1865. In 1866 he played for Yorkshire against Nottinghamshire at Bradford, then travelled to Nottingham to turn out next day against Nottinghamshire again, but this time for Middlesex! Father of C. T. A. Wilkinson, the Surrey captain in 1914 and 1919–20.

INDEX

coach, value as 13, 17, 202
media and 54–5
Insole, Doug 99, 139–40, 148–9
International Cavaliers 139
International Cricket Conference
(ICC) 90, 93, 97, 101, 139, 140,
141, 146, 148

Jackman, Robin 106, 109, 146
Jardine, Douglas 86
Jarvis, Paul 136–7, 141, 171, 195
Jeacocks, Alfred 46
Johnson, Colin 47, 163
Johnson, Peter 47–8
Johnston, Brian 129
Jones, Alan 188
Jones, Dean 2, 87
Jubilee Test 117

Kanhai, Rohan 139
Kent 42, 80, 152
Kenyon, Don 139
Khan, Imran 85, 96, 97, 100
Khan, Shakeel 52, 97
Kilburn, J.M. 47
Kingston 111
Kirk, Reg 167, 169, 182
Knott, Alan 13, 17

Lahore 52
Lampitt, Stuart 191
Lancashire 47, 172, 178
Larkins, Wayne 108
Larwood, Harold 85, 86
Lawrence, David 12
Lawson, Geoff 89
Leadbetter, David 17
league cricket
deterioration of 34
Leeds City Council 166
Leeds Cricket, Football and
Athletic Club 33, 166, 172, 216
Leicestershire 16, 35, 81, 124, 126,
214

Lendl, Ivan 17
Lenham, Les 13
Lever, Peter 48, 156
Lewis, Tony 129
Leyland, Maurice 74
Leyton 46
Lillee, Dennis 16, 31, 62, 66, 67,
80, 85, 98, 100, 123, 202
Lilleshall 22
Linacre, Sir Gordon 168
Lindwall, Ray 85
Lister, Joe 47, 151, 168, 171
Lloyd, Andy 12
Lloyd, Clive 47, 78
Lloyd, David 14
Lord's 39, 40, 45, 49, 65, 67,
77, 110, 112, 142, 182,
189, 191, 214
Love, Jim 185, 200, 205
Lumb, Richard 39
Lush, Peter 52, 113

McEnroe, John 99
McEwan, Steve 191
McKenzie, Graham 80
Mail on Sunday 130
Malcolm, Devon 7, 8, 15
Mann, George 146
Marlar, Robin 146
Marsh, Rodney 202
Marshall, Malcolm 59, 63, 78, 210
MAST (Management and Skills
Training) 158–9
Matthews, Sir Stanley 99
Maxwell, Robert 50
May, Peter 3, 7, 51, 68, 139, 187
Maynard, Matthew 12
Metcalfe, Ashley 18, 171, 194,
195, 207–8
Meyer, Barrie 49
Miandad, Javed 98
Middlesex 18, 20, 51, 65, 77, 152
Miller, Geoff 88, 114, 116
Miller, Keith 85

Mitchell, Arthur 19–20, 41, 60, 194
Moscow Olympics 136
Mosey, Don 55, 217
Motz, Dick 155
Mountgarret, Viscount 160, 162, 163, 167, 168, 169, 170, 171, 172, 175–6, 176, 177, 178, 179, 214
Moxon, Martyn 78, 171, 191, 195, 202, 205, 207–8, 212–13
Murdoch, Rupert 50
Mutch, Duncan 146, 184–5

Nash, John 41
National Cricket Association 12
NatWest Trophy 18, 34, 35, 121, 209
New South Wales Cricket Association 122
Newport, Phil 191
Nicholson, Tony 26
night Test cricket 101
Northamptonshire 6, 16, 146, 151, 163
Northern New South Wales 108
Nottinghamshire 25, 51

O'Keeffe, Kerry 108
O'Neill, Norman 187–8
Old, Chris 15, 114, 119, 154, 157, 202, 205, 206
Oldham, Steve 18, 202, 204, 212
one-day cricket 24, 34–5
Orange Free State Cricket Union 143
overseas players
county cricket and 31–2, 33

Packer, Kerry 21, 85, 101, 149
Padgett, Doug 18, 30, 193–5, 202, 204
Palmer, Ken 39–40, 97
Pamensky, Joe 140, 149

Parfitt, Peter 77
Parker, Paul 12
Parkinson, Sir Kenneth 163
partnerships 85
Pascoe, Len 39, 62, 66, 92
Piggott, Tony 12
pitches
condition of 94–5
TCCB and 27–8, 30
uncovered 28–9, 30
Platt, Bob 163, 165, 185, 198
Pocock, Pat 206
Pollock, Peter 85
Pridgeon, Paul 191
Pringle, Derek 191
Procter, Mike 39–40, 63–4, 85

Qasim, Iqbal 88
Quinn, Peter 161, 176

racism
Yorkshire and 16
Radford, Neil 12
rain
uncovered pitches and 28–30
Ramprakash, Mark 7, 18–19
Ramsey, Sir Alf 22
Rana, Shakoor 52, 97, 98
Randall, Derek 62
Regis, John 134
Rhodes, Steve 206
Rice, Clive 210, 212
Richards, Viv 49, 71–2, 73, 87, 92, 100, 105, 110, 111, 118, 148
Roberts, Andy 66, 72, 81
Roberts, Tony 176
Robinson, Phil 195
Robinson, Tim 3
Robson, Bryan 54
Roche, Tony 17
Roebuck, Peter 71, 142
Row, Raman Subba 52, 139, 140, 141
Russell, Eric 21